"*A Decision to Love* is a first-rate resource for use with virtually any marriage preparation program, whether a single-session model, a series of evenings, or a weekend. John and Susan include resource and discussion materials on every key aspect of marriage, and their insights on how to present the content in ways suitable for engaged couples is right on the money. Any engaged couple who uses this material will be fortunate, indeed."

Mitch Finley
Author, *Married Love: A Special Way of Being Alive*

"*A Decision to Love* manages to put into perspective a fact often overlooked by engaged couples: the wedding is one day in our lives, the honeymoon, perhaps a week. Engagement is not a preparation for that brief period; it is a time to prepare for the rest of our lives.

"In the hands of a skillful leader, this program will give a loving relationship the tools needed for survival. After twenty-two years of my own marriage, we are just beginning to discover many of the issues raised in this thoughtful and well-written book. All couples—engaged, newly married, and not so newly married—will find food for thought, topics for discussion, and issues still needing clarification in the helpful workbook sections.

"This is excellent—an answer to prayer for many parishes."

Kathleen Chesto
Author, *Family Spirituality*

"John and Susan Vollmer Midgley bring their considerable pastoral experience and personal insights to the task of marriage preparation in this new book. They confront the major issues of the day (substance abuse, AIDS, dual career couples) as they invite engages couples to discuss honestly the many aspects of married life. *A Decision to Love* will be a valuable resource to parishes in their ministry with engaged couples."

Paul Covino
Pastoral Ministry Consultant
Upton, Massachusetts

"What a joy to discover *A Decision to Love*. There lies in these pages a carefully crafted resource and communication tool, ideal for marriage preparation, but also valuable for many years into marriage. This gem is packed with timely information, designed to be practical. The layout and exercises are highly conducive to communicating, listening, sharing. There is a sensitive and caring spirit pervading this work of love, giving it a spiritual yet practical flavor that very much resembles marriage itself. All who use this material are likely to find direction and wisdom in their love's journey."

Lawrence J. Losoncy, Ph.D.
Licensed Marriage-Family Therapist
Tulsa, Oklahoma

D1316489

Leader's Guide
(Includes Couple's Book)

A Decision to Love
A Marriage Preparation Program

John M.V. Midgley

Susan Vollmer Midgley

TWENTY-THIRD PUBLICATIONS
Mystic, Connecticut 06355

Second printing 1993

Twenty-Third Publications
185 Willow Street
P.O. Box 180
Mystic CT 06355
(203) 536-2611
800-321-0411

ISBN 0-89622-538-0
Library of Congress Catalog Card Number 92-61349

Acknowledgments

Pages 42, 44: "The Johns Hopkins Twenty Questions: Are You an Alcoholic?" Courtesy of Johns Hopkins University Hospital. Used with permission.

Pages 50–51: "Different Directions" by John Denver. © 1991 Cherry Mountain Music. All rights reserved. Used by permission.

Pages 61, 63: *Traits of a Healthy Family.* © 1983 by Dolores Curran. Courtesy of Harper-SanFrancisco. Used with permission.

Pages 125–151: Excerpts from the English translation of *Rite of Marriage* © 1973, International Committee on English in the Liturgy, Inc. (ICEL); excerpts from the English translation of *The Roman Missal* © 1973, ICEL. All rights reserved. Used with permission.

Pages 126–139: *The Jerusalem Bible.* Copyright 1966, 1967, 1968 by Darton, Longman & Todd Ltd and Doubleday, a division of Bantam, Doubleday, Dell Publishing Group, Inc. Reprinted by permission of the publisher.

Contents

Information Boxes

A Decision to Love

Introduction

Welcome to the leader's guide of *A Decision to Love*. Because you are part of a marriage preparation team, you have a deep concern for the health and well-being of the engaged couple's future marriage. You are investing your time, talent, and emotional and psychological energy into this. It's a big investment, but the returns are priceless.

You will find that being part of a marriage preparation process can be exciting, stimulating, beautiful, exhausting, frustrating, and scary. It's exciting to observe a young couple discover something new about themselves. It's stimulating to your own relationships to have other married couples give talks on communication skills and other topics. It's beautiful to have an engaged couple thank you at the end of a program for what you've done for them. It's exhausting to have to leave home on an evening or weekend, arrange for a sitter, rush off to church at the end of a long day to be with couples who may not want to be there in the first place. It's frustrating when the program doesn't run as well as you think it should. And it's scary to see what impact your words may have on the engaged couples who hear them.

A Decision to Love

This workbook is entitled *A Decision to Love* because we believe that loving and being loved is a decision. Real love is not something that just happens once and never changes. Rather, because we are always growing and changing, our love has to grow and change. Keeping that love alive and renewed demands much from us: First, it demands a commitment to our love; second, it demands a belief that the love is worthwhile; and finally, it demands a decision to continue loving, even when we may not feel lovable or may not feel like loving anyone.

God's decision to create, sustain, and love us is the model of all love, which is to love unconditionally and fully. Jesus is our model in this; he walked among us, and taught us through his example about love. As married couples, we are called to this kind of love and to this kind of decision. Jesus' life and love have challenged us to learn to give love to our partners with the fullness and depth that we are loved by God.

Leader's Guide

This leader's guide that accompanies the engaged couple's edition is meant to assist you in running a marriage preparation program. It includes (in reduced form) all the pages found in the engaged couple's book as well as further suggestions on running a program. It also contains exercises that are not in the couple's edition. Since this edition is also meant to be a planning guide, we have included notes to assist you with the planning of your marriage preparation program.

Purpose of Marriage Preparation

Why have you volunteered to help couples prepare

for their marriage? Your answer to this question will be personal, but it has to include the fact that the overall purpose for marriage preparation is to help couples prepare for a marital relationship that will be a life-giving journey of love, hope, and faith. As the title of this workbook indicates, we believe marriage is based on a decision that a couple makes to love each other. This decision is not made once and for all, but is an on-going, growing, and maturing decision that has to be reaffirmed every day in the couple's life together.

Engaged couples typically are so romantically "in love" with each other that they are not initially receptive to the idea of love as a decision. They may think it just "happens" to them. They see love purely as an emotion, which at this time in their lives is overflowing. In this workbook we attempt to affirm this, but also to encourage them to move beyond that stage and mature in their love.

Flexibility of Workbook

A Decision to Love is designed to fit into any new or existing marriage preparation program. It is not designed as an entire program in itself; thus it allows you greater flexibility to meet the needs of the program that you may already be running in your parish or diocese. Later in this volume, for those who are just beginning a program or looking for new ideas in an existing one, we suggest ways to run a marriage preparation program.

If you decide to use *A Decision to Love* in your already existing program, we suggest that you carefully select from it the chapters and the material in each chapter that you intend to use in your program. There are in this book eight chapters, a wedding liturgy planning section, information boxes of useful information, and a resource appendix that cover much more material than the typical marriage preparation program allows for. Encourage your engaged couples to complete, on their own at a later time, whatever material you do not cover in your program.

His Pages and Her Pages

In all the chapters of *A Decision to Love*, you will find a His Page and a Her Page, with the same questions in each. Allow enough time for each person to answer the questions on his or her page and to discuss their answers together. These pages should be removed from the couple's book to allow each the opportunity to answer the questions privately. The couple should then confer with each other, comparing their answers.

Some questions are open-ended, requiring answers of some length; some are closed-ended, requiring short answers: multiple choice, true or false, and fill-ins. This variety is intentional, since every individual will prefer one style over another. Marriage preparation coordinators across the country have reported that people in marriage preparation programs are about evenly divided in their preference.

If the amount of time available during your program is a concern, consider assigning only the short-answer and multiple choice questions to the couples. They should be encouraged, however, to answer the remaining questions later on their own.

Case Studies and Group Discussions

You will find various group questions and case studies throughout *A Decision to Love*, including several "baby cases" in Chapter 6. We have found case studies to be useful in small group discussions. If you decide to use the material in this way, here are a few suggestions.

First, in leading a small group discussion on a case study, the golden rule is that there are no wrong answers. A good case study is open to interpretation, analysis, and an exchange of opinions. Correcting someone when he or she expresses an opinion will discourage any further desire to share an opinion. Allow a free flow of possibilities for each case study. If your small group seems to reach a premature "solution," they should be challenged to look at other possibilities.

Another point to remember in your small group discussions is that no one should ever be pressured into saying something. You can encourage a quiet individual to speak by a friendly glance or nod. Or you may ask a non-threatening, open-ended question in order to elicit some response. In any event, respect their desire to be silent, if that is their choice.

Questionnaires and Exercises

There are various questionnaires, exercises, and ice-breakers found in the couple's edition and this leader's edition. Chapters 2, 3, and 4 in particular offer a variety of resources you can offer the couples in your program.

Information Boxes

A feature of *A Decision to Love* is the many information boxes found throughout the book, featuring topics such as cohabitation, AIDS, pre-marital counseling, dual-career couples, interfaith marriages, co-dependency, alcoholism and addictions, fighting, in-laws, remarriage, divorce, jealousy, spouse abuse, living with parents and natural family planning. These brief information boxes may serve as discussion starters, thought provokers, and supplemental aides to presentations given in your marriage preparation program. The table of contents lists all of these boxes and the page where each one may be found.

Issues of Special Focus

In the couple's edition you will also find boxes with questions targeted for couples with special issues to deal with, such as pregnancy, previous marriage, stepchildren, significant age difference, and older couples. There is no specific space given in the workbook for writing answers to these special focus questions. During your program, encourage the engaged to read these questions and, during the breaks or on their own time, discuss any that may pertain to them.

Relationship Check

Each chapter ends with a relationship check. It is important for engaged couples to get an over-all assessment of how they feel after each chapter's topic. Stress the importance of this exercise. Couples are often amazed that after a certain topic is covered, one of the two of them may not be comfortable with their answers and discussions and may want to pursue the subject further. A glance back over the chapters at the end of the program will highlight for the engaged couples the topics that may still need work.

Planning of the Wedding Liturgy

A section on planning the wedding liturgy is also included in the couple's edition. If time and interest allow, it is often a good idea to go through this with the engaged couples. Most of them have never participated in planning a liturgy before, and they may be feeling somewhat lost and overwhelmed at this time. This is a good opportunity for you to get couples thinking about their wedding day and how their liturgy will be a symbol, an expression, of their Christian marriage.

All prayers, responses, and reading options for the ceremony are presented in the planning section, including two copies of the Planning Sheet (a draft copy and a final copy) so the couple can prepare a final list of all the decisions they make regarding their wedding ceremony.

Resource Appendix

The last information found in this workbook is an extensive listing of self-help and referral resources. During an encounter such as a marriage preparation program, some individuals will come upon personal issues in their lives that they may want assistance dealing with. This resource list offers national 800, or hotline, numbers and addresses of groups they may be interested in. If you observe that a couple appears unusually troubled by a presentation or exercise, you may want to simply ask if everything is all right and make yourself available to them before or after the program or during breaks. If it's appropriate, you may wish to refer them to a professional. No marriage preparation team couple is ever asked to take on a role they are not qualified to assume. We also recommend that you have local numbers for these groups or for professionals in case a couple requests assistance.

Certificates

At the completion of any marriage preparation program, certificates should be administered as (1) a way for the couple to verify their participation and completion of the program to their parish priest or minister, (2) a way of acknowledging the effort and investment they made in the program, and (3) a tangible sign to the couple that their engagement is something important to you, the team, and the church. See pages 5 and 6 for examples.

If you do not already have a design for your marriage preparation certificate, you may want to choose one of the following models. We recommend you photocopy them on colored, heavy paper.

Ice-Breakers

We suggest you start a marriage preparation program with some type of warm-up exercise. If your program has several sessions, consider having such an exercise at the beginning of each session if time permits. Some of the exercises listed throughout the couple's edition and leader's edition may be used in such a capacity. Or you may want to use the following exercises.

1. Who's Married to Whom? (for large group; beginning of program). Have all the team preparation couples stand up front, men on one side in a row, women on the other side. Have the engaged couples attempt to match up the partners, or have each small group attempt it and then see which small group had the most correct. Make sure that none of the engaged see any of the team members standing with their spouse.

2. Couple to Couple (small group ice-breaker). Have two engaged couples interview each other, and then introduce each other to the other couples in the group. Each should find out the following information from the other couple: their names, town(s) of residence, wedding date, honeymoon plans, their favorite pastime as a couple, and the like.

3. Is That Me? (small group ice-breaker). Have each person write on a piece of paper their partner's:

> favorite color
> favorite season of the year
> favorite sport or hobby
> favorite song
> eye color
> whether their big toe is longer than the toe next to it.

The papers are then handed in to each small group team leader, without names on them and without their partners seeing the answers. The team leader then mixes them up, and reads them out loud one at a time. Each person is then to guess which of the set of answers describes them.

Suggestions for Conducting a Marriage Preparation Program

Most dioceses and churches have well formulated policies and procedures regarding the marriage preparation process within their boundaries. That is why *A Decision to Love* is a flexible workbook, adaptable to most pre-existing programs, and not a prepackaged program in itself. There is no need to re-invent the wheel if you already have a smooth running marriage preparation structure in place. If, however, you are looking for ways to improve your marriage preparation program or if you are in fact just initiating such a program, we offer the following ideas for your consideration.

Basic Marriage Preparation Structure

The basic cycle of most pre-Cana programs consists of a presentation on a given topic by a trained married couple (team couple), followed by an exercise or worksheet for each engaged couple to do and discuss among themselves, followed by a small group exercise. This cycle is repeated, each time focusing on a different topic such as communication, spirituality and religion, finances, and sexuality. This cycle can and should be mixed with various ice-breakers, group exercises, and couple exercises.

Two models for a marriage preparation program using *A Decision to Love* are suggested on pages 8-9.

We encourage you to have the engaged couples sit in small group circles of four or five couples, plus one team couple. This serves three purposes: (1) such an arrangement is better for a more informal and warm atmosphere as opposed to having an auditorium style arrangement; (2) it allows for potentially greater interaction between couples and at least one of the team couples; (3) small group interaction complements the presentations and couple interaction that the engaged are experiencing in your program.

This is to certify that

_____

(bride)

and

_____

(groom)

have completed
A Decision to Love
marriage preparation program.

_____   _____

(date)   (coordinator/priest)

CERTIFICATION

_____ and _____
(bride)   (groom)

have completed the marriage preparation for

_____
(diocese/parish/agency)

_____   _____
(date)   (coordinator/priest)

Use name tags during the program. Couples may complain or joke about this kind of "labeling," but the tags help in developing a sense of connectedness and involvement in the program.

A fitting way to end your marriage preparation program is with some type of prayer service. We offer a sample service later in this workbook.

Presentations

Most marriage preparation programs incorporate presentations by the team couples on the following or similar topics: communication, dealing with disagreements, spirituality and religion, finances, and sexuality. These are the core topics to be covered in any program. You will find outlines for these at the end of Chapters 2, 5, 7, 8. Beyond these, you may want to consider having presentations on the following: family of origin, personality differences, natural family planning, children and parenting, wedding liturgy planning.

Ideally, a presentation is given by one of the team couples, and should last no longer than 20 minutes. The key to a successful talk is for the team couples to be well prepared, relaxed, and genuine. Do not pretend to be something you aren't, or to know something you don't. Be yourself! The talk should reflect your own lived experience as a married couple, struggling and loving through life. You don't have to be a "pro" on the subject you're presenting.

A presenting couple wins over the engaged couples if they state at the beginning of their talk words similar to the following: "We're not professionals. We don't have all the answers. But we are a married couple who cares. We're here to share with you some of our experiences and insights on the subject of...."

One-Day
Marriage Preparation Program
(Model 1)

9 A.M. Registration. Coffee and donuts.

9:30 Welcome. Opening prayer. Introductions of team members.

Use of an ice-breaker ("Who's Married to Whom?" for example). Explanation of the purpose of the program. Odds and ends (location of bathrooms, smoking policy, etc.).

10:00 Small group ice-breaker, or blind partner exercise.

10:20 Couple exercise: *A Decision to Love*, pages 7-10 (Chapter 1)

10:40 Presentation by team couple: Communication

11:00 10 minute break

11:10 Couple exercise: *A Decision to Love*, pags 15-18 (Chapter 2)

11:30 Small group exercise: *A Decision to Love*, Case Study, page 14 (Chapter 2)

12:10 P.M. Lunch

12:45 Couple exercise: *A Decision to Love*. Engaged couple chooses one of the exercises and/or sets of questions from Chapters 3 and 4.

1:15 Presentation by team couple: Sexuality

1:35 Couple exercise: *A Decision to Love*, pages 51-54 (Chapter 5)

1:55 5 minute Break

2:00 Small group questions: *A Decision to Love*, page 55 (Chapter 5) and/or small group baby cases, page 63 (Chapter 6)

2:45 Presentation: Finances

3:05 15 minute break, snacks

3:20 Couple pages: *A Decision to Love*, pages 69-73 (Chapter 7)

3:55 Presentation: Spirituality

4:15 Couple pages: *A Decision to Love*, pages 79-82

4:40 Small group exercises: *A Decision to Love*, page 83

5:00 Prayer service

5:30 Dinner (optional)

Three-Evening
Marriage Preparation Program
(Model 2)

First Evening

6:45 P.M. Registration

7:00   Welcome. Opening prayer. Introductions of team couples
            Explanation of the purpose and procedures of the program. Odds and ends

7:15   Small group ice-breaker

7:30   His and Her Pages: *A Decision to Love*, pages 7-10 (Chapter 1)

7:45   Small group discussion questions: page 11 (Chapter 1)

8:00   Presentation by team couple: Communication

8:20   His and Her Pages: *A Decision to Love*, pages 15-18 (Chapter 2)

8:35   Break

8:40   Small group exercise: *A Decision to Love*, Case Study, page 14
            and group section questions: page 19

9:00   Presentation by team couple: Personalities and Separate Pasts

9:15   Couple exercise: *A Decision to Love*, pages 25-32 (Chapter 3)

9:30   Closing remarks

Second Evening

7:00 P.M. Welcome back. Old business

7:05   Presentation: Family of Origin

7:25   His and Her Pages: *A Decision to Love*, pages 41-44 (Chapter 4)

7:40   Small group exercise: Case study, page 45

7:55   Break

8:00   Presentation: Sexuality

8:20   His and Her Pages, pages 51-54 (Chapter 5)

8:40   Presentation: Children

9:00   His and Her Pages: pages 59-62 (Chapter 6)

9:15   Small group exercise: Baby cases, page 63

9:30   Closing remarks

Third Evening

7:00 P.M. Welcome back. Old business

7:05   Presentation: Finances

7:25   His and Her Pages: pages 69-72 and Our Section, page 73 (Chapter 7)

7:45   Presentation: Spirituality

8:05   His and Her Pages: pages 79-82 (Chapter 8)

8:25   Break

8:30   Planning the wedding liturgy

8:50   Evaluations and questions

9:00   Prayer service

9:30   Closing remarks

Concluding Prayer Service

Requirements: Small white taper candles, 1 per person; large white pillar candle (possibly the church's Paschal Candle) placed up front.

Priest/
Team Couple: Lord Jesus, you have told us that whenever two or more are gathered in your name, that you are there with them. (*pause*) Lord, we thank you for the gift of love. We thank you for this opportunity to come together, in love, to find out more about ourselves and you. We ask you to strengthen us as a couple, in your love. This we ask through you, our Lord.

All: Amen.

Reader: An appropriate Scripture reading; for example:

John 17:20-23	Matthew 22:35-40	John 2:1-11
John 15:9-12	1 John 4:7-12	1 Corinthians 12:31-13:8

Priest/
Team Couple (*Instructing the engaged couples with words similar to the following*): For our unity candle ceremony, we ask that one person from each small group come up to the Paschal Candle, light his or her candle, and return to the group where the others will light their candle from that one.
(Dim the room lights and light the large Paschal Candle. Distribute the small taper candles to each group, one per person.)

Priest/
Team Couple (*as the Paschal Candle is lit*): Lord Jesus, you are the light of the world. Come into our lives, and show us the way.

(Pause. Briefly invite the group representative to come forward to light his or her candle and then return to light the candles of the group members.)

Music: *During this part of the ceremony, some appropriate music should be played on a tape player in the background. A soft instrumental piece works well or a gentle hymn from a Christian musician such as John Michael Talbot, The St. Louis Jesuits, David Haas, Weston Priory.*

Priest/
Team Couple (*after the song and every candle is lit*): In the midst of the darkness of our daily problems and stresses, God softly comes to us as a light of hope and love. Our God is a God of gentleness, of humor, of invitation, of embracing. May we follow our God and build our relationship on hope, love, gentleness, and humor. (*pause*)
   Come, Lord Jesus, and light our path. For the journey of marriage is long and sometimes dark, but we are filled with hope because you are with us in our life together.
(Turn the room lights back on. Briefly instruct the couples to blow out their candles. Keep the Paschal Candle lit.)

Priest/
Team Couple: Now let us join hands and pray in the words that our Savior taught us...."

All: Our Father, who art in heaven....

Our Decision to Love

Of all the chapters in *A Decision to Love,* this may be the one some team leaders will tend to drop or ignore in their preparation program. Please don't! We find that it is very important for engaged couples to look at the what, why, how, when, and where of their coming together as a couple. The material in this chapter helps the couple to focus on the story of their relationship so far. They are challenged to view their marriage as a mature, Christian *decision* to love.

Whether the engaged man and woman have known each other for ten years or three months, each needs to reflect on their beginning as a couple, which most couples want to do. Because of this, you may want to assign some of the exercises in this chapter as a warm-up at the start of your program.

Depending on the individual maturity of each partner, they may already have a good grasp of the realities of life-long marital love and commitment. Even so, you want to make sure that they are seeing beyond the rose-colored glasses of new love. The Group Section is good in bringing up common cliches and ideas that need to be challenged.

You may want to inform yourself about such things as pre-nuptial agreements, and pre-marital cohabitation. These topics may surface in a small group discussion. As a team, decide beforehand how you want to respond to topics such as these. We recommend that you also find out what the official position of your diocese is on these topics.

Notes

Chapter 1
Our Decision to Love

They would have celebrated their second anniversary today. But instead, Sherry finds herself alone. It's hard to figure what went wrong. Somehow, after the wedding everything changed. She discovered so much she hadn't known about Tom. And when it came to the important things, like sharing the chores or having a baby, she realized they hadn't talked about them or agreed upon anything at all. It had felt so wonderful to be in love, who wanted to talk about things that might create hard feelings or cause a fight? She hoped that everything would just kind of work itself out later.

Thinking about it, Sherry remembers the married team couples at her marriage preparation class saying again and again ". . . engagement is the time to make sure you are ready to marry. It is never too late to wait or to take more time. Be honest with each other. Don't hold anything back. Relationships take work." With a sad smile she remembers how she used to imitate them, to Tom's great amusement, mocking the advice she suspected might be right. Maybe she hadn't been ready. Maybe Tom wasn't her Mr. "Right." But what was she to do after all those years of dating, be alone again? Anyway, the wedding had been planned for months. She wanted to get married.

Now it was clear she had been wrong. If she had known then what she knew now about Tom, herself, and their marriage, she would have taken the advice of those couples and taken a harder look at their relationship before they got married. She would have been more honest, less afraid to talk about what was really bothering her. Maybe Tom

Note: This page is reproduced from the Couple's Book.

would have done the same. Maybe they could have worked it out. Maybe, maybe, maybe, Sherry thinks. Maybe they could have been celebrating their second anniversary now, together and in love, instead of waiting, each of them alone, for their divorce to be finalized.

Finding Mr. or Ms. "Right" is something we all hope for. Children are raised with "Snow White" or "Cinderella" stereotypes firmly in mind. The Princess-in-distress is rescued by a stunning young Prince who loves her, after which they live happily ever after.

While these images are indeed fairy tale ones, most people unconsciously expect their lives to go in a similar way. When we ask couples in marriage preparation classes what happened when they fell in love, most say it just kind of happened, that it was magical, and that it happened when they weren't quite looking. It was wonderful, a time filled with excitement over plans and the future. These feelings and thoughts about falling in love and about engagement are important to every couple who experiences them. But they need to be balanced with a little reality and some concrete conversations about what your marriage will be like. Excitement and plans don't carry a relationship through the challenges and hard times. Only love with a solid foundation can do that.

Common among engaged couples is an unrealistic expectation we refer to as the myth of marital determinism. It presupposes that the success of your marriage is determined by finding that one right person for you. If you don't happen to find that special partner, then a life of unhappiness and/or divorce is inevitable. But if you do find Mr. or Ms. "Right," a life of joy and peace is sure to follow. One of the many problems with this deterministic view is that when rough times do occur in your marriage, you may be more inclined to view your marital troubles as an indication that you did not find the "right" person. And instead of trying to work together on your relationship, you'll simply agree to break up because "it was a big mistake from the start."

The truth is that there is not just one person in this world for you. There are obviously many people with whom you could be married. But you have *chosen* this one person. A life-

---

PRE-NUPTIAL AGREEMENTS

A Pre-Nuptial Agreement is a legal contract between two individuals engaged to marry each other, which states in detail how assets will be divided if they divorce in the future. Some see such an agreement as a good insurance policy. But in reality, it may be more of a self-fulfilling predictor of doom. For a couple about to marry in the church, who are about to make a lifelong decision to love in good times and bad, in sickness and in health, for richer or poorer, Pre-Nuptial Agreements may be seen as courting disaster.

The Catholic church has no official teaching regarding such premarital contracts. But, as one priest who works with couples seeking annulments stated, such an agreement at the time of engagement can be construed as a lack of seriousness by the couple toward the permanence of their commitment. There is a sort of "bail out of it if it gets too hot" mentality behind it, and it undermines the need for the engaged couple to seriously consider the commitment they are about to make.

If your partner approaches you with a request to sign such an agreement, especially if it's right before the wedding . . . Beware! "Honey, I'll love you forever, but please sign on the dotted line."

Note: This page is reproduced from the Couple's Book.

COHABITATION

"The overall association between premarital cohabitation and subsequent marital stability is striking," states a 1987 study by the National Bureau of Economic Research. The authors of the study were shocked to find that couples who live together before marrying have close to an 80 percent higher divorce rate than couples who don't cohabit. These findings, substantiated by other independent studies, point to a reality in sharp contrast to commonly-held beliefs of "trial marriages." The fragility of the post-cohabitation marriage was the surprising result of the research for demographers, sociologists, economists and therapists.

There are many reasons why couples cohabitate. Many couples do it for financial reasons, others do it for the convenience. Some couples are engaged to be married, others are attempting to see if they're compatible. Some couples who live together are not sexually active with each other. And others live together as a trial marriage.

A 1983 National Council on Family Relations study of over 300 newly-married couples found a higher level of dissatisfaction among those couples who lived a trial marriage before their wedding. Women, in particular, were more unhappy with the quality of communication with their spouses after they married. But why is this the case? And, more importantly, why do couples who live together before marriage have a higher divorce rate?

No one knows for sure. But probably one of the main reasons is that those couples who view premarital cohabitation as a trial marriage are deceiving themselves. As someone once said, living together before marriage in order to prepare for marriage is like taking a bath in order to prepare to swim the English Channel. The best way to prepare for marriage is to talk with each other about every aspect of your relationship, your own personalities, and your future goals. Oddly enough, it seems that premarital cohabitation actually inhibits such basic communication.

time of happiness together is not based on chance or on a sort of predetermined cosmic blueprint; rather it is based on the two of you making a mature, Christian decision to love each other...on the day of your wedding, and every day of your married life.

The decision to marry is a *decision to love*. It's not magic. It's not a roulette game of chance. It's not always easy. Some days the last thing in the world you will want or feel like doing is loving your partner. But those are the days that you say to yourself, "Today, I decide to love my partner." A decision to love demands maturity, selflessness, and a true sense of self-respect.

No couple is 100 percent compatible or perfect for each other. To make your marriage work, you will have to work on it, some days more than others.

This first chapter will focus on your being together and your decision to stay together. Your stories of how you met, and all the details surrounding it, are important because they are the first bricks in the foundation of your relationship and upcoming marriage.

It's important to reflect on the fact that you chose one another and to share with each other the thoughts and feelings associated with it. It is also just as important to look at how those initial feelings and thoughts will affect your future together and your ability to make a lifelong commitment.

In all the chapters of this workbook, we challenge you to challenge yourself and your partner. We encourage you to take this time seriously, to be honest and patient with each other. It is our hope that through these exercises you will discover new things about yourself, your partner, and your relationship which will strengthen your bond and commitment. But since there are some sensitive and often difficult questions, we also realize that there may be times when you will feel shaky and unsure about one or more of these topics. That's O.K. Your engagement is supposed to be the time during which you look at your relationship, discovering those areas that aren't perfect and may require some work. So take your time with this and allow yourselves the opportunity to start your marriage off on the right foot.

6

Note: This page is reproduced from the Couple's Book.

His Page

Answer these questions by yourself and then share your answers with your partner.

1. What did I like about you when we first met?_____

_____

_____

2. What did I dislike about you?_____

_____

_____

3. How did you make me feel about myself when we were together?_____

_____

_____

4. What did I first like about us as a couple?_____

_____

_____

5. What did we decide about living together before marriage and why? How do I feel about our decision?_____

_____

_____

6. What made us decide to marry? How do I feel about that?_____

_____

_____

7. Going from being single to being married requires a change in lifestyle. In which of these areas do I think I will need to make changes? In which do I think you will need to make changes?

	ME	YOU	WHY?
Time spent with friends	☐	☐	_____
How money is spent	☐	☐	_____
Hours at work	☐	☐	_____
Leisure time	☐	☐	_____
Time spent with family	☐	☐	_____

7

Note: **This page is reproduced from the Couple's Book.**

8. What have we decided about a pre-nuptial agreement?_____
_____
_____

How do I feel about that?_____
_____
_____

How will our decision affect our relationship?_____
_____
_____

9. Who are the people that I feel have helped and supported us as a couple?_____
_____
_____

Who do I think have exceptionally good marriages? Why? _____
_____
_____

10. When I dream about our future, this is what I see in 3 years: _____
_____
_____

in 10 years: _____
_____
_____

Note: **This page is reproduced from the Couple's Book.**

Her Page

Answer these questions by yourself and then share your answers and reflections with your partner.

1. What did I like about you when we first met?_____
_____
_____

2. What did I dislike about you?_____
_____
_____

3. How did you make me feel about myself when we were together?_____
_____
_____

4. What did I first like about us as a couple?_____
_____
_____

5. What did we decide about living together before marriage and why? How do I feel about our decision? _____
_____
_____

6. What made us decide to marry? How do I feel about that?_____
_____
_____

7. Going from being single to being married requires a change in lifestyle. In which of these areas do I think I will need to make changes? In which do I think you will need to make changes?

	ME	YOU	WHY?
Time spent with friends	☐	☐	_____
How money is spent	☐	☐	_____
Hours at work	☐	☐	_____
Leisure time	☐	☐	_____
Time spent with family	☐	☐	_____

9

Note: This page is reproduced from the Couple's Book.

8. What have we decided about a pre-nuptial agreement?_____

_____

_____

How do I feel about that?_____

_____

_____

How will our decision affect our relationship?_____

_____

_____

9. Who are the people that I feel have helped and supported us as a couple?_____

_____

Who do I think have exceptionally good marriages? Why? _____

_____

_____

10. When I dream about our future, this is what I see in 3 years:_____

_____

in 10 years: _____

_____

_____

<u>10</u>

Note: This page is reproduced from the Couple's Book.

ISSUES OF SPECIAL FOCUS

If these issues pertain to you, discuss them with your partner.

1. How will our coming together affect our children?

How do they feel about me? you?

Do they feel a part of our new marriage?

2. How do I feel about your children?

How do I feel when I am with them?

3. Have we discussed adopting each other's children?

Do I think that I will feel like a real mom/dad to them?

What do we expect from each other as parents?

4. If there is more than eight years difference in our ages, how do I feel about this?

How will this affect our relationship?

5. If you've already been married by a Justice of the Peace or in another church, why are you coming to the Catholic church to have your marriage convalidated?

GROUP SECTION

Answer these questions as a couple and then discuss your answers with other couples in your group.

1. When you hear the phrase "love at first sight" what do you think of?
   Do you agree or disagree with this statement?
2. Do you believe that "opposites attract"? Why?
3. Define "commitment." How do you feel about making a commitment?
   What, if any, are the conditions?
4. What do you think about pre-nuptial agreements?
   Do you think they effect a couple's ability to make and keep a commitment? Why?

RELATIONSHIP CHECK

Each of you should circle the number that best represents how you feel about your relationship after discussing these topics. Remember, you each need to select your own number.

   1. very close   2. somewhat close   3. somewhat distant   4. very distant

What do I want to discuss further with you?

_____
_____
_____
_____
_____
_____

Note: This page is reproduced from the Couple's Book.

Chapter 2

Our Communication/Negotiation

Good communication practices, and in particular good negotiation skills, are necessary in a good marital relationship. In earlier generations it was just as important, but in some ways it was less difficult and complex than it is today. A couple today is more distracted from home life, less likely to assume the traditional roles in which everyone pretty much knew what was expected. Because they are so busy, they are more likely to spend their time and energy on other people and things than on each other. Therefore, the engaged couples you encounter may need help in focusing their attention and energy on each other, on their relationship.

This chapter offers a variety of ways to help you help the engaged couple. You will find His and Her Pages, Our Section, Group Section, a Case Study, Special Focus Questions, and some Information Boxes. Of particular interest is the "Rules for Disagreements" tear out. You may want to suggest to them that they post it on their refrigerator.

You may also want to consider the following two exercises, called "The Maniac" and "Communication Takes Two," for the presentation on communication and negotiation. The first one is an excellent way to illustrate how perceptions can differ from one person to another, and thus affect our communication.

"The Maniac"
At the end of the presentation on communication,

but before the presenting couple sits down or gives any final words, have one of the other team members jump up and go through a series of fast-paced, disjointed activities in front of everyone. The presenting couple should just step back, stop presenting, act surprised like everyone else, and observe with the rest of the group. "The maniac" could do the following nonsensical activities:

- Jump up and down 3 times
- Run to the light switch and flick the lights off and on 4 times
- Run to one of the seated team members and shout "9, 6, 3, 6, 7"
- Run to an empty chair, sit down, and clap his or her hands 5 times
- Stand up, raise one leg, and shout, "Four score and six years ago..."

And so on.

As a team, figure out the maniac's script ahead of time. Have fun with it! The more details, actions, and weird statements the maniac makes, the better. The group of engaged couples will obviously be in a state of disbelief, or laughing, depending on how much of a comic the maniac is. But they will catch on to what just happened when the presenting couple tells them what to do next.

They are to write down, in detail, in order of sequence, and with the exact number of times, all the things the maniac did and said. Give them 5 minutes to do this; they are not to talk. Then have them discuss in their small groups their perceptions of what happened, the differences in their perceptions. The key is that everything the maniac did was choreographed, and each team couple has a copy of the script which will help the engaged couples compare the reality of what happened with their perceptions of it.

Point out to the small groups that there was only one reality, but several perceptions and interpretations of what happened. So it is in marital communication: perceptions are often more important than what actually is said or done! We must always confirm what we think we just saw or heard to make sure it's right.

"Communication Takes Two"

For this exercise, you'll need to photocopy the figures on page 23, which are to be distributed to one member of each couple. Be careful that the other member does not see the figures as they are handed out. The purpose of this exercise is to demonstrate that better communication takes place when it's a give and take. One-way communication is ineffective, at best. Two-way communication, although not perfect, makes any task easier.

The person with the photocopy sheet is to describe Figure 1 to his or her partner, who will attempt to draw it. They are to sit back to back. The one who is drawing is not allowed to ask any questions, nor communicate in any way with the partner. After 5 minutes, announce that everyone is to stop Figure 1 and start Figure 2. For this they are allowed to sit facing each other, and the draw-er is allowed to ask questions. Again, allow 5 minutes and then stop the exercise. Then have each couple look over the figures and drawings together and discuss their difficulities of doing Figure 1 and the relative ease of doing Figure 2. This brief exercise is fun and worthwhile. Try it!

Figure One

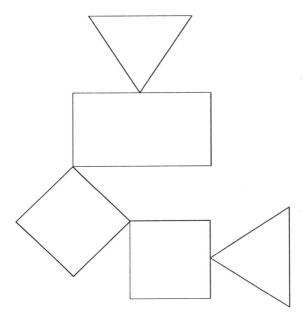

Instructions: Put your chairs back to back, so you cannot see each other. You are then to describe how to draw the figure above to your partner without using your hands, and without showing your partner the drawing. No questions are allowed from your partner. Start with the top figure and work your way down.

Figure Two

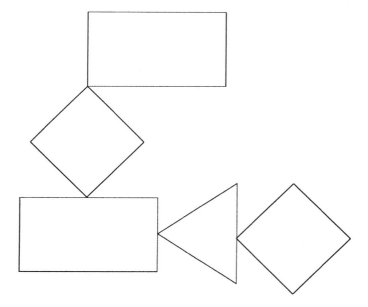

Instructions: Turn your chairs around and face each other. You are to describe how to draw the figure above to your partner. You are allowed to use your hands, and your partner is allowed to ask questions.

Our Communication/Negotiation
Talk Outline

1. Introduce self and topic
- Number of years married?
- Any children? Ages?
- Town you live in? Church?
- How long involved as marriage preparation volunteers?
- Any other general information about yourselves?
- What's your topic?
- Why is it important for the engaged couples to hear about this topic?

2. Communication as an art
- Most people assume it just happens naturally.
- Communication is an art requiring practice, energy, attention, skills, patience, and love.
- "Talking is cheap," but true communication is priceless!

3. Communication involves the verbal and the nonverbal
- Talking is verbal communication.
- Active listening, body language, facial expressions, tone of voice, hand gestures, eye contact are all examples of nonverbal communication.
- Nonverbal communication is very important and powerful.
- When there is a conflict between verbals and nonverbals in messages being sent, the receiver will tend to trust the nonverbal message over the verbal message!

4. In a close interpersonal relationship, such as marriage, one of the trickiest types of communication is the "resolution of conflict"—in other words, "fighting"
- Fighting does not have to be *bad,* *"destructive,"* or *hurtful.*
- Fighting can be *good,* *"constructive,"* and *helpful.*
- Society teaches and provides models for destructive fighting techniques: e.g., yelling, abuse, mind games, silent treatments, name-calling, accusations, threats, etc. All of these are based on the "winner" vs "loser" mentality.
- In your marriage, there should be no winner—no loser. If one of you "wins" an argument, both of you lose.

5. Review the rules for disagreements, "refrigerator copy"

NOTES:
1. Read the couple's and leader's edition chapters on this topic.
2. Lace all talks with personal examples, stories, and real life anecdotes that add color and/or demonstrate what you are talking about.

Notes

Chapter 2
Our Communication/ Negotiation

On his way to work, Carl uses his cellular car phone to remind his secretary at the office to fax certain reports to Chicago. Pam, already at her job, checks the electronic mail on her computer terminal for any messages regarding the teleconference she will attend later that day. At work, Carl and Pam epitomize modern, sophisticated users of high-tech telecommunications. At home, they are more old-fashioned.

Last night, Carl and Pam had another of their yelling matches on the same old recurring themes: he doesn't listen to her, she nags him. After the argument, he marched off in a silent rage, and she burst into tears. You see, Carl and Pam also epitomize today's young married couple who doesn't know how to communicate.

All around us we notice that in the use of slick telecommunication, today's society is futuristic, light-years ahead of its time. And yet when it comes to interpersonal communication, we often trudge along like grunting cave dwellers.

Communication between a husband and wife is an absolute necessity! But communication involves more than just the mouth and the ears. It involves the total person: eyes, hands, mind...heart. Communication between you and your partner cannot incorporate the cold transmission of information, as it does when Carl is on his cellular car phone or Pam is at her computer terminal. True communication between loving partners must involve, on both sides, a warm sharing of self. It must involve the total giving of yourself to your partner.

Note: **This page is reproduced from the Couple's Book.**

Effective interpersonal communication does not come easily. It requires certain skills that don't come naturally and are therefore often overlooked. These skills need to be learned. Because people in our society are poor at negotiating differences and haven't actually learned any good ways to do it, they often resort to negative behaviors such as yelling, abuse, defensive attitudes, silent treatments, or cheap verbal shots. In the world outside your marriage, these techniques will classify you as aggressive at worst. In the world of your marriage, they may destroy the relationship. Destructive fighting tears down, destroys, takes life away. Constructive fighting builds up, enhances, gives life to the marriage.

We have two little boys. And we're constantly amazed at how many bumps, bruises, and scrapes they get. But we're even more amazed at how fast the "boo-boos" heal. Their young bodies quickly recuperate. Though we're not ancient, we notice that on our bodies such scrapes and bumps take a lot longer to heal. And individuals in the twilight years of their lives realize that some bruises never heal.

Your marriage is similar. While it's still very young, it has an amazing capacity for self-mending. The two of you are able to bounce back from a destructive fight relatively quickly, and the fight leaves no apparent scar. But as your marriage matures, its resilience diminishes. Scars form. Repercussions from destructive fights remain.

This is why it is very important to establish good skills for fair fighting now while your marriage is young. Disagreements are inevitable, even necessary for a strong, lasting relationship. But they can be expressed in a life-giving and constructive way. If you are practicing destructive fighting techniques now, chances are you will begin to develop more lasting scars.

FIGHT!

Often people assume fighting is bad. Actually, for an intimate, exclusive relationship such as marriage, fighting not only has the potential to be good, but is also necessary. But in order for the fighting to be good for the relationship, it must be constructive and not destructive.

A constructive fight is a "fair" fight in which both sides win. A good way to determine the quality of your fighting is to ask yourself: "How do I feel about myself after we fight?" It's not a question of whether you got your way or "won" the fight. Rather, it's a question of whether the process you both used to negotiate your differences is "life-enhancing" to you and your relationship. If you feel put-down, guilty, revengeful, manipulated or manipulative, hateful, or smug after you've fought, then chances are your fighting is taking a destructive toll on your relationship.

Constructive fighting should build up, enhance, fortify, and actually nurture your relationship, regardless of who "wins." The following is a good process for dealing with your differences that may enable your fighting to be life-enhancing and not life-taking from your relationship.

The next time you have a disagreement, sit down and face each other. Using the Rules for Disagreements in this chapter, take turns stating your side of the issue. However, before voicing your views, you must restate the ideas and feelings expressed by your partner and do so to the satisfaction of your partner. This is difficult to do. The assumption here is that if I can tell you what you said and felt, then I truly heard and understood you. If I can't, then either I was not fully present to you while you spoke, or else you were not sufficiently clear. This process of fighting motivates each of you to clarify your thoughts before you speak and to concentrate on what your partner is truly saying and not on what your response is going to be.

"LISTEN"

The Chinese written word for "listen," *ting*, is a composite of four other words: *er - dr* (ear), *tu -lau* (mind), *yen - jin* (eye), and *shem* (heart). The combination of these four vital parts leads to effective listening. We must not only hear with our ears, we must also listen with our minds, our eyes, and our hearts.

Note: This page is reproduced from the Couple's Book.

In this chapter we will focus on how well you think you communicate as a couple. The questions will reflect this focus, and will also ask you to look at how you fight. We have also listed some tried and true rules for disagreements; you can tear this page out and hang it on your refrigerator.

One final note. We have found that one of the best ways to witness your partner's true colors before you marry is to have a fight of substantial weight. We don't mean a little nagging, recurring squabble, but a serious disagreement. Too often engaged couples avoid discussing an issue they know will erupt into a fight, hoping that somehow the wedding will make it all O.K. We think that this is a mistake. We're not advocating that you fabricate a fight just because we suggest it will help your relationship! Rather we are saying that you should not avoid fighting before the wedding (or after the wedding). When you're angry, upset, or hurt, and you attempt to communicate that to the one you love, your true self emerges. Facades tumble. Pretenses vanish. How you "look" is no longer important. You're hurt or angry and you want your partner to know it! If you don't like what you see in your partner or yourself when you fight, then you probably won't like what you see in your marriage down the road. The quality of your fighting now, before you marry, may indicate the quality of your future marriage.

CASE STUDY: BILL AND CHRISSY

"I'm furious at you! You made me feel foolish at the pizzeria! Why did you do that?" Chrissy demands. Bill, with a little grin on his face, calmly responds. "Listen, I was only joking. Everyone knew I wasn't serious when I said that you talked so much that my ears hurt. Besides, everyone laughed. You always blow things out of proportion!"

"You jerk!" she explodes. "You think you're so smug. How would you like it if the next time we're with our friends I 'joke' about your problems with your mom?"

"You'd better not!" Bill says sternly. "Besides, I don't think you fully understand that situation yourself!" He stroms off to the car and drives away.

What makes this fight such a destructive one? Why do each of them say and do things that are unfair and hurt the other?

Note: **This page is reproduced from the Couple's Book.**

His Page

Answer these questions by yourself and then share your answers with your partner.

1. I think that I communicate with you:

☐ very well   ☐ well   ☐ not as well as I could   ☐ poorly

How does my answer make me feel? _____

_____

2. I think that you communicate with me:

☐ very well   ☐ well   ☐ not as well as you could   ☐ poorly

How does my answer make me feel? _____

_____

3. What was the last big decision we made together? _____

_____

Who made the decision? _____

4. How did we come to the decision? _____

_____

_____

5. Am I happy with how decisions are made in our relationship, or are there things I would like to see changed? Explain _____

_____

_____

6. If we couldn't come to a decision that both of us agreed upon, what would we do?
☐ I would decide.   ☐ You would decide.   ☐ We would forget about the whole thing.
☐ We would go ask someone else.   ☐ We would compromise.
☐ Other_____

_____

7. I can always tell when you are angry because _____

_____

_____

15

Note: This page is reproduced from the Couple's Book.

8. When we have a big fight, what do we each do?

	ME	YOU		ME	YOU		ME	YOU
yell	☐	☐	become sarcastic	☐	☐	hit partner	☐	☐
become silent	☐	☐	make a joke out of it	☐	☐	talk about how we feel	☐	☐
cry	☐	☐	say insulting things	☐	☐	listen	☐	☐
walk off	☐	☐	bring up past issues	☐	☐			
throw/hit things	☐	☐	don't listen	☐	☐			

9. What was our last argument about?_____
_____

Do I think that you understood my side?_____
_____

Do I think that I understood your side?_____
_____

10. When I am angry with you, I _____
_____
_____

11. Whenever we fight, you make me feel _____
_____

12. The topics that usually start a fight between us are:

a._____
_____

b._____
_____

13. When you cry, I feel _____
_____

14. Do I ever fear that you will become violent and hurt me? Explain_____
_____
_____

_____
16

Note: This page is reproduced from the Couple's Book.

Her Page

Answer these questions by yourself and then share your answers with your partner.

1. I think that I communicate with you:

☐ very well   ☐ well   ☐ not as well as I could   ☐ poorly

How does my answer make me feel? _____

_____

2. I think that you communicate with me:

☐ very well   ☐ well   ☐ not as well as you could   ☐ poorly

How does my answer make me feel? _____

_____

3. What was the last big decision we made together? _____

_____

Who made the decision? _____

4. How did we come to the decision? _____

_____

_____

5. Am I happy with how decisions are made in our relationship, or are there things I would like to see changed? Explain. _____

_____

_____

6. If we couldn't come to a decision that both of us agreed upon, what would we do?
   ☐ I would decide.   ☐ You would decide.   ☐ We would forget about the whole thing.
   ☐ We would go ask someone else.   ☐ We would compromise.
   ☐ Other _____

_____

7. I can always tell when you are angry because_____

_____

_____

17

Note: This page is reproduced from the Couple's Book.

8. When we have a big fight, what do we each do?

	ME	YOU		ME	YOU		ME	YOU
yell	☐	☐	become sarcastic	☐	☐	hit partner	☐	☐
become silent	☐	☐	make a joke out of it	☐	☐	talk about how we feel	☐	☐
cry	☐	☐	say insulting things	☐	☐	listen	☐	☐
walk off	☐	☐	bring up past issues	☐	☐			
throw/hit things	☐	☐	don't listen	☐	☐			

9. What was our last argument about?_____
_____

Do I think that you understood my side?_____
_____

Do I think that I understood your side?_____
_____

10. When I am angry with you, I _____
_____
_____

11. Whenever we fight, you make me feel _____
_____

12. The topics that usually start a fight between us are:

a._____
_____

b._____
_____

13. When you cry I feel_____
_____

14. Do I ever fear that you will become violent and hurt me? Explain. _____
_____
_____

_____
18

Note: This page is reproduced from the Couple's Book.

OUR SECTION

Discuss and answer these questions together as a couple.

1. What couple do you know who you both think demonstrates good communication skills? You must agree here. If you can't agree on a couple, why not?

2. In what ways do you think you could communicate better? Talk about changes that each of you is willing to make.

ISSUES OF SPECIAL FOCUS

If these questions pertain to you, discuss them with your partner.

1. Do I like the way I communicate with my children? Your children?

2. How do the children handle their anger toward me? You?

3. How were anger and disagreements handled in my/your previous marriage? What would I like to see different this time?

GROUP SECTION

Discuss these questions with a group of other engaged couples.

1. What are some "mind games" couples play when they're fighting? (Examples: trying to make your partner feel guilty, waiting for your partner to ask you if there is something wrong, or denying that there is a problem to be talked about.)

2. What do you think is meant by this statement: A couple needs to communicate not only with their ears and mouth, but also with their hearts, their heads, and their souls?

3. In many homes people communicate through sarcasm, teasing, and violence. How can you avoid these behaviors? Discuss why they are destructive.

RELATIONSHIP CHECK

Each of you should circle the number that best represents how you feel about your relationship after discussing these topics. Remember, you each need to select your own number.

    1. very close   2. somewhat close   3. somewhat distant   4. very distant

What do I want to discuss further with you?

_____
_____
_____
_____
_____

19

Note: **This page is reproduced from the Couple's Book.**

RULES FOR DISAGREEMENTS
(Refrigerator Copy)

1. Use "I" Statements and Avoid "You" Statements

I put you on the defensive if I start my sentence with "You…"

2. Use "Heart" Statements and Avoid "Head" Statements

I will tell you how I feel (not what I think). Please understand that my feelings are mine, that I have a right to them…and don't judge them.

3. Don't Interrupt

In this way, I will not only "hear" you, but I will truly "listen" to you and try to understand your view without rushing in with my own views. Then, please listen to me without interrupting.

4. Don't "De-personalize" the Fight

I will maintain eye contact with you. I will stop whatever else I am doing (like watching TV). I will not call you names, or trivialize your view by making a "joke" out of it. I will sit down with you and talk it through. I won't walk out, unless we both agree to cool down for awhile. Please treat me with the same respect.

5. Fight Lovingly

I understand that "fighting" and "loving" are not necessarily different. Even in my anger and rage, I love you. I promise that even in the midst of our fighting, I will not say or do anything that will belittle or destroy you or our relationship. Please deal with me and our relationship in the same nurturing way.

6. Keep It Simple

I will try as hard as possible to be clear and stick to the issue at hand. Because I may be emotional, angry, or hurting, it may be difficult for me to talk. But I promise to try. If nothing else, I will tell you, "I feel angry" or "I feel hurt." I ask you to also be clear and to not bring up past issues.

7. Don't Play Mind Games

I will always try to be direct and sincere with you; I will not play games or fool with the "trust" and "honesty" that our relationship is built on. I ask that you try to be direct with me too, avoiding any mental or emotional games.

8. Don't Abuse

I realize that I know things about you that no one else knows. I know what topics are sensitive to you. I know your weak spots. I promise not to abuse this almost-sacred knowledge I have. I promise not to abuse you. I ask that you not abuse me, for I too am vulnerable to you.

9. Don't Be Afraid to Seek Professional Help

If our fighting happens more often and increases in its intensity and we feel that our differences are becoming unmanageable, then let's contact a counselor. I realize that we may feel foolish, embarrassed, or unsure as we seek this help. But I also realize it's better to err on the side of caution than to watch our marriage die.

20

Note: This page is reproduced from the Couple's Book.

Chapter 3

Our Separate Pasts and Personalities

How many times have you heard a married person (or yourself) observe, "It's the little things in marriage that build up to be big things....and big problems"? Whether it's the socks left in the middle of the floor, the toothpaste tube squeezed in the middle, the forgotten anniversary, or the amount of television watched, the "little" annoyances in any close relationship can lead to fights, anger, and negative feelings if not dealt with in a healthy way.

This chapter helps the engaged couple examine how they are different. They realize that not only are they different, but that their differences are often based on the fact that they are two different personalities with two different histories.

The Personality Assessment is an enjoyable and enlightening exercise. Typically when the couples are comparing their answers you'll hear some laughter and joking, which is good. But you may also hear and see some serious discussions going on. Couples are sometimes amazed by how they see each other and themselves. After the Personality Assessment, you may want to present the case study of Kevin and Emily for a small group discussion.

The Alcoholism Questionnaire is something you may want to recommend they complete on their own time, at home. Point out the Resource Appendix in the back of their book. And have on hand the local numbers for Alcoholics Anonymous (A.A.), Narcotics Anonymous (N.A.), and Al-Anon.

"Familiarity breeds contempt."

Aesop

"Familiarity breeds contempt—and children."

Mark Twain

"Though familiarity may not breed contempt, it takes the edge off admiration."

William Hazlitt

Kevin and Emily

In the Personality Assessment, Kevin rated himself, in order, as Mother Teresa, St. Francis, Teddy Roosevelt, Leonardo Da Vinci, and Mickey Mouse. Emily rated Kevin in order as the Statue of Liberty, Peter Pan, Archie Bunker, Evil Knevil, and Leonardo Da Vinci. Assuming that neither Kevin nor Emily are 100 percent correct in their assessments of Kevin, what do they need to talk over about their personality reviews of Kevin? How does Kevin see himself? How does Emily see Kevin? What is the overall picture that they each paint of Kevin? How are they different? How are they the same?

Notes

Chapter 3
Our Separate Pasts and Personalities

"Flannel shirts! I love flannel shirts. I'm a flannel shirt type of guy. Well, she doesn't like flannel shirts! She wants me to walk around the house in dress shirts all day. In fact, she threw out all my flannel shirts!" Stephen was becoming increasingly upset as he relived story upon story of how Megan, his wife of only one year, was attempting to change him. "The other day, we got into a big fight after a party," he continued. "Miss 'Life of the Party' over there was angry at me because I wanted to come home early. Heck, I was tired!"

"Well, if you weren't such a bump-on-a-log, if you could just loosen up once in awhile," she shouted back, "then maybe you'd have some fun too!"

Megan was trying to change not only how he dressed, but how he spoke, how he carried himself in public, how he planned things, even how he thought. She was trying to mold him into something he was not. She was doomed to fail, of course. But, unfortunately, she didn't realize that she was also dooming his trust in her.

21

Note: **This page is reproduced from the Couple's Book.**

And Stephen, likewise, was attempting to subdue Megan's spirited personality.

Often the very characteristics that first attracted us to our partners are the very characteristics we eventually attempt to change. Opposites may attract . . . but familiarity also breeds contempt. And this often leads to attempts at making your partner more like you.

When they first started dating, Megan and Stephen's opposite personalities balanced each other well. Megan found Stephen's quiet, introverted ways a source of comfort and rest from her hectic pace as an emergency room nurse. And he was attracted to Megan's energetic and outgoing approach to life. However, after a year of marriage, Megan wished Stephen wanted to go out more with their friends, and Stephen wished Megan would slow down and cool it once in awhile.

We're happy to report that five years later, after some marriage counseling and a lot of hard work, Megan and Stephen are happily married. When they look back over their years of turmoil, they agree that the biggest lesson they learned is that you cannot change another person. People change only if they want to.

This chapter will focus on your different personalities. "Oh, but we're so much alike," you may say. Well, unless you're marrying a clone of yourself, the two of you are different. No two people are completely compatible. To one degree or another, you and your partner are incompatible. And many of your differences are based on the simple fact that you, as individuals, have different personalities. Not to acknowledge your partner's unique personality is to deny your partner the respect he or she deserves.

What do we mean when we say that you have different personalities? Quickly, answer these questions to yourself: Which one of you is more outgoing and social? Which one is more organized? More emotional? More stubborn? More confident? More idealistic? More romantic? More financially minded? You see, you are different. And it's surprising how the "little" differences between you now can grow into "big" differences down the road.

While dating, he may find it cute how she absentmindedly

CO-DEPENDENCY

An alcoholic has an uncontrollable dependency on alcohol; a drug addict has a dependency on drugs; a compulsive gambler depends on gambling. A co-dependent is someone who has a "dependency" on someone else, usually a loved one who is an alcoholic or addict of some type. The common link between all of these dependencies, whether on a substance, a behavior, or a person, is the unhealthy obsessive/compulsive behavior that consumes the dependent individual.

Alcoholism and addictions affect not only the alcoholic or addict, but everyone close to this person. Co-dependency refers to the maladaptive behavior, the irrational thinking, and the suppressed but intense feelings that take place as a result of the addiction of a loved one. Co-dependents stop living for themselves. Co-dependents become more and more enmeshed in the bizarre world of the addict. Co-dependents may even take the responsibility for the alcoholic's drinking, and may believe that if they only did "this" or "that," the person would stop drinking.

Co-dependents may believe they can cure or control the addiction but may subconsciously facilitate it by denying the problem and helping to hide it from neighbors, parents, or the boss.

Co-dependents are not happy people. Their obsession with the alcoholic's drinking or the addict's unhealthy behavior overrides all other thoughts, feelings, plans, goals, all enjoyment in life. A co-dependent, like the addicted person, leads a dysfunctional life. And after awhile, the co-dependent suppresses all personal needs and feelings. We have stressed elsewhere and will emphasize here, if you find yourself in such an unhealthy situation, seek professional counseling. It may be one of the most loving and healthy things you can do for yourself, your partner, and your relationship.

Note: This page is reproduced from the Couple's Book.

misplaces her keys. Or she may find him attractive when he aggressively takes control of a situation. But after a year or two of marriage, of constantly misplaced items and aggressive behavior, the cuteness and attractiveness of their differences may become problematic. And each may attempt to change the other.

In their book *Please Understand Me*, David Keirsey and Marilyn Bates contend that the primary source of fractured marriages is a phenomenon they call "The Pygmalion Project." This refers to the attempts of some spouses to transform their partners into copies of themselves. They write: "It is as if the marriage license is construed as a sculptor's license, giving each spouse the warrant to chisel away until the other becomes the spit and image of the sculptor."

You cannot change your partner. Look at him or her long and hard...because what you see now is basically what you'll have 10, 15, 40 years from now. Your partner will obviously change a little, but his or her basic personality will remain the same. And if your partner does change, it will have to be your partner's decision, not yours.

Included in this chapter is a short his and her personality assessment that will introduce you to your own personality traits and those of your partner. It has been designed to be an enjoyable, non-threatening way for you to think about and discuss your differences and similarities. The events of our pasts are an important part of who we are and can therefore have an effect on our relationships. Like personalities, they too are something that cannot be altered. When left undiscussed, the events of our past have potential to become a source of conflict.

Old boyfriends, girlfriends, spouses, and families of origin are permanent chapters in your book of life. For that reason, this chapter will also focus you and your partner on your individual pasts and invite you to share more about them with each other. We believe that by sharing about your past before you are married, you are saving your partner and your relationship from any surprises or old patterns of behavior that will eventually surface. Honesty is a crucial component for a successful marriage.

Finally, if abuse (drug or alcohol, physical or emotional),

SPOUSE ABUSE

Spousal abuse, especially wife abuse, is considered to be the most common unreported crime in the U.S. Approximately twenty million women are repeatedly abused by men whom they know. Worse, only about 10 percent of all abuse cases are reported to authorities.

What is spouse abuse, or battering? It's the repeated subjecting of one person to any forceful physical or psychological behavior by another without any regard for her or his rights. Battering doesn't develop overnight. There are usually early indicators of potential wife or husband abuse.

1. Does your partner ever go into a rage of unreasonable anger?

2. Is your partner physically violent?

3. Does your partner have a poor self-image?

4. Does your partner abuse alcohol or drugs?

5. Were you or your partner physically abused as a child?

6. Does your partner consistently blame you for his/her problems?

7. Do you find yourself rationalizing or justifying your partner's anger or violence?

If your answer is "yes" to any of these questions, seek professional counseling before you marry. If physical abuse is already present in your relationship, then call off the wedding now! Things will not get better. They will get worse! For further guidance, contact a counseling agency or a local advocacy group for battered women.

Note: This page is reproduced from the Couple's Book.

addictions (gambling, overeating, drugs, alcohol, sex, spending), mental illness, or other unusual behaviors have been a part of your life or your family's past or present, talk to your partner about it now. *Seek help if you find your behavior is beyond your control.* And if your partner has a problem, encourage him or her to seek help too. Problems such as these don't go away. They only get worse. Don't delude yourself with thinking that your love or this marriage will make it all O.K. While love and marriage might serve as temporary distractions, problematic behavior will drag you along with it and destroy your marriage in the process.

ALCOHOLISM/SUBSTANCE ABUSE

1. Addiction to alcohol and drugs (illegal and prescription) is much more common and widespread than most of us realize.

2. Alcoholism is a disease! It's not the result of weak will power, poor moral character, or some deficient personality.

3. Alcoholism does not discriminate....anyone can have the disease: females and males, whites and blacks, poor and rich, young and old!

4. There is no cure for alcoholism or any addictions. If you are an addict, you will always be an addict. Total abstinence from alcohol and drugs for alcoholics and drug abusers is the only way to stop the effects of these addictive behaviors.

5. Addictions are extremely powerful! Denial of the problem by the addicted person and loved ones is the common way of dealing with such an overwhelming problem.

6. Self-acceptance is the first step toward recovery. Active and on-going participation in support groups are crucial to the addict's recovery.

7. Addictions not only affect the addict, but also the addict's loved ones, both family and friends. They too need to seek support and help from groups such as Al-Anon and Ala-Teen.

8. Alcoholism is a progressive disease and, like all addictions, leads ultimately to death.

9. An active addict will stop at nothing to continue the addictive behavior.

10. Often family members will subconsciously adapt their behavior, thinking, and feelings to accommodate the addicted person's bizarre behavior. This is known as co-dependence. People who are co-dependent need to seek help for themselves.

24

Note: This page is reproduced from the Couple's Book.

His Personality Assessment

From the following list, pick five or more "characters" that you feel reflect your personality the best. Rank them in order from 1–5, with 1 being the most like you. Then do the same for your partner. Don't let the gender of the character determine your selections. Rather, let the images they suggest guide you.

Me You
- ☐ ☐ PETER PAN: perpetual child
- ☐ ☐ GUMBY: flexible
- ☐ ☐ STATUE OF LIBERTY: "Let me show the way"
- ☐ ☐ BAMBI: meek and gentle
- ☐ ☐ GENERAL PATTON: takes control
- ☐ ☐ OSCAR THE GROUCH: pessimist, sour
- ☐ ☐ MOTHER TERESA: saves the world
- ☐ ☐ ALBERT EINSTEIN: scientist
- ☐ ☐ ST. FRANCIS: back to nature
- ☐ ☐ DON JUAN: romantic
- ☐ ☐ BOY SCOUT: trustworthy
- ☐ ☐ GEORGE WASHINGTON: "never tell a lie"
- ☐ ☐ CHARLIE BROWN: loner
- ☐ ☐ RAMBO: "take no prisoners"
- ☐ ☐ SNOOPY: party animal
- ☐ ☐ EVIL KNEVIL: thrill seeker
- ☐ ☐ TEDDY BEAR: soft and cuddly

Me You
- ☐ ☐ DONALD TRUMP: business
- ☐ ☐ TEDDY ROOSEVELT: "talk softly and carry a big stick"
- ☐ ☐ MICKEY MOUSE: "Fun! fun! fun!"
- ☐ ☐ ARCHIE BUNKER: opinionated
- ☐ ☐ RHETT BUTLER: "I don't give a damn"
- ☐ ☐ DEAR ABBEY: problem solver
- ☐ ☐ FRED FLINTSTONE: loud
- ☐ ☐ FRANK LLOYD WRIGHT: the architect
- ☐ ☐ SANDRA DAY O'CONNOR: the judge
- ☐ ☐ LEONARDO DA VINCI: artist
- ☐ ☐ MISS MANNERS: "a proper way for everything"
- ☐ ☐ SADDAM HUSSEIN: mother of all pretenders
- ☐ ☐ HENRY KISSINGER: negotiator
- ☐ ☐ GEORGE BURNS: the comic
- ☐ ☐ BOZO: the clown
- ☐ ☐ ROBERT FROST: the poet

DISCUSS YOUR "CHARACTERS"

Now compare the characters that you have selected for yourself and for your partner and discuss them. Use these to get your discussion started:

1. Discuss each character and why you or your partner selected it.

2. Do you feel that your partner's selections correspond with the way you see yourself? Why?

3. Do these characters paint an overall picture of each of you?

4. Do any of these characters point out behaviors that you or your partner might want to change?

25

Note: **This page is reproduced from the Couple's Book.**

His Alcoholism Questionnaire

This test, used by Johns Hopkins University Hospital in Baltimore, is helpful in determining whether someone has a drinking problem.

Answer these questions (yes "y" or no "n") for yourself and your partner as best you can. Compare your answers with your partner's. Each question may also be used to determine drug addiction by replacing "drinking" with "doing drugs."

Me You

☐ ☐ Do you lose time from work due to drinking?
☐ ☐ Is drinking making your home life unhappy?
☐ ☐ Do you drink because you are shy with other people?
☐ ☐ Is drinking affecting your reputation?
☐ ☐ Have you ever felt remorse after drinking?
☐ ☐ Have you gotten into financial difficulties as a result of drinking?
☐ ☐ Do you turn to lower companions and an inferior environment when drinking?
☐ ☐ Does your drinking make you careless of your family's welfare?
☐ ☐ Has your ambition decreased since drinking?
☐ ☐ Do you crave a drink at a definite time daily?
☐ ☐ Do you want a drink the next morning?
☐ ☐ Does drinking cause you to have difficulty in sleeping?
☐ ☐ Has your efficiency decreased since drinking?
☐ ☐ Is drinking jeopardizing your job or business?
☐ ☐ Do you drink to escape from worries or trouble?
☐ ☐ Do you drink alone?
☐ ☐ Have you ever had a complete loss of memory as a result of drinking?
☐ ☐ Has your physician ever treated you for drinking?
☐ ☐ Do you drink to build up your self-confidence?
☐ ☐ Have you ever been to a hospital or institution on account of drinking?

If you have answered YES to any one of the questions, there is a definite warning that you may be an alcoholic. If you have answered YES to any two, the chances are that you are an alcoholic. If you have answered YES to three or more, you are definitely an alocholic.

Unfortunately, the abuse of alcohol, drugs, sex, food, gambling, and spending is becoming increasingly more common in today's world. The effects of this abuse are devastating to the individual caught in the negative behavior and to those people who love the abuser.

As an engaged couple, you should look seriously and honestly at any area in your lives that might point out behavior that is out of control. The following behaviors may indicate serious problems: frequent drunkenness from alcohol or highs from drugs; promiscuity; use of pornography or inappropriate sexual behavior; food binges or crash diets; spending large amounts of money on races, slot machines, or lotteries; and sky high credit card usage or shopping binges.

If any of these fits either you or your partner, stop and talk about it. Get help! Don't try to pretend that the problem is not there. Be honest with yourself and your partner and get help in order to get your life back under control. Marriage will not change these behaviors.

26

Note: **This page is reproduced from the Couple's Book.**

Her Personality Assessment

From the following list, pick five or more "characters" that you feel reflect your personality the best. Rank them in order from 1–5, with 1 being the most like you. Then do the same for your partner. Don't let the gender of the character determine your selections. Rather, let the images they suggest guide you.

Me You
☐ ☐ PETER PAN: perpetual child
☐ ☐ GUMBY: flexible
☐ ☐ STATUE OF LIBERTY: "Let me show the way"
☐ ☐ BAMBI: meek and gentle
☐ ☐ GENERAL PATTON: takes control
☐ ☐ OSCAR THE GROUCH: pessimist, sour
☐ ☐ MOTHER TERESA: saves the world
☐ ☐ ALBERT EINSTEIN: scientist
☐ ☐ ST. FRANCIS: back to nature
☐ ☐ DON JUAN: romantic
☐ ☐ BOY SCOUT: trustworthy
☐ ☐ GEORGE WASHINGTON: "never tell a lie"
☐ ☐ CHARLIE BROWN: loner
☐ ☐ RAMBO: "take no prisoners"
☐ ☐ SNOOPY: party animal
☐ ☐ EVIL KNEVIL: thrill seeker
☐ ☐ TEDDY BEAR: soft and cuddly

Me You
☐ ☐ DONALD TRUMP: business
☐ ☐ TEDDY ROOSEVELT: "talk softly and carry a big stick"
☐ ☐ MICKEY MOUSE: "Fun! fun! fun!"
☐ ☐ ARCHIE BUNKER: opinionated
☐ ☐ RHETT BUTLER: "I don't give a damn"
☐ ☐ DEAR ABBEY: problem solver
☐ ☐ FRED FLINTSTONE: loud
☐ ☐ FRANK LLOYD WRIGHT: the architect
☐ ☐ SANDRA DAY O'CONNOR: the judge
☐ ☐ LEONARDO DA VINCI: artist
☐ ☐ MISS MANNERS: "a proper way for everything"
☐ ☐ SADDAM HUSSEIN: mother of all pretenders
☐ ☐ HENRY KISSINGER: negotiator
☐ ☐ GEORGE BURNS: the comic
☐ ☐ BOZO: the clown
☐ ☐ ROBERT FROST: the poet

DISCUSS YOUR "CHARACTERS"

Now compare the characters that you have selected for yourself and for your partner and discuss them. Use these to get your discussion started:

1. Discuss each character and why you or your partner selected it.
2. Do you feel that your partner's selections correspond with the way you see yourself? Why?
3. Do these characters paint an overall picture of each of you?
4. Do any of these characters point out behaviors that you or your partner might want to change?

27

Note: **This page is reproduced from the Couple's Book.**

Her Alcoholism Questionnaire

This test, used by Johns Hopkins University Hospital in Baltimore, is helpful in determining whether someone has a drinking problem.

Answer these questions (yes "y" or no "n") for yourself and your partner as best you can. Compare your answers with your partner's. Each question may also be used to determine drug addiction by replacing "drinking" with "doing drugs."

Me You

- [ ] [ ] Do you lose time from work due to drinking?
- [ ] [ ] Is drinking making your home life unhappy?
- [ ] [ ] Do you drink because you are shy with other people?
- [ ] [ ] Is drinking affecting your reputation?
- [ ] [ ] Have you ever felt remorse after drinking?
- [ ] [ ] Have you gotten into financial difficulties as a result of drinking?
- [ ] [ ] Do you turn to lower companions and an inferior environment when drinking?
- [ ] [ ] Does your drinking make you careless of your family's welfare?
- [ ] [ ] Has your ambition decreased since drinking?
- [ ] [ ] Do you crave a drink at a definite time daily?
- [ ] [ ] Do you want a drink the next morning?
- [ ] [ ] Does drinking cause you to have difficulty in sleeping?
- [ ] [ ] Has your efficiency decreased since drinking?
- [ ] [ ] Is drinking jeopardizing your job or business?
- [ ] [ ] Do you drink to escape from worries or trouble?
- [ ] [ ] Do you drink alone?
- [ ] [ ] Have you ever had a complete loss of memory as a result of drinking?
- [ ] [ ] Has your physician ever treated you for drinking?
- [ ] [ ] Do you drink to build up your self-confidence?
- [ ] [ ] Have you ever been to a hospital or institution on account of drinking?

If you have answered YES to any one of the questions, there is a definite warning that you may be an alcoholic. If you have answered YES to any two, the chances are that you are an alcoholic. If you have answered YES to three or more, you are definitely an alocholic.

Unfortunately, the abuse of alcohol, drugs, sex, food, gambling, and spending is becoming increasingly more common in today's world. The effects of this abuse are devastating to the individual caught in the negative behavior and to those people who love the abuser.

As an engaged couple, you should look seriously and honestly at any area in your lives that might point out behavior that is out of control. The following behaviors may indicate serious problems: frequent drunkenness from alcohol or highs from drugs; promiscuity; use of pornography or inappropriate sexual behavior; food binges or crash diets; spending large amounts of money on races, slot machines, or lotteries; and sky high credit card usage or shopping binges.

If any of these fits either you or your partner, stop and talk about it. Get help! Don't try to pretend that the problem is not there. Be honest with yourself and your partner and get help in order to get your life back under control. Marriage will not change these behaviors.

Note: **This page is reproduced from the Couple's Book.**

His Page

Answer these questions by yourself. When you are finished discuss your answers and reflections with your partner.

1. Do I feel that you are trying to change me? How?_____
_____
_____
_____

2. How do I think that our personalities compliment each other?_____
_____
_____
_____

3. How do I feel about discussing my past relationships? Can I be honest? Do I think that you really listen to me and understand?_____
_____
_____

4. How do I feel about discussing your past relationships?_____
_____
_____

5. Am I concerned about my use of drugs or alcohol? spending habits? sexual activity? eating? or gambling?
_____
_____

6. Do I feel in control of these behaviors? Explain._____
_____
_____

7. When you are in a bad mood I usually...

☐ try to make you feel better   ☐ fix it   ☐ ignore you   ☐ feel bad

☐ offer to listen   ☐ give you your space

8. Do I think that I am responsible for your feelings?_____
_____
_____

9. Am I concerned about your use of drugs or alcohol? spending? sexual activity? eating? or gambling?
_____
_____
_____

29

Note: This page is reproduced from the Couple's Book.

10. Have I ever felt that any of these behaviors is out of control in your life? Explain._____

_____

_____

11. Do I feel that we need to discuss the use of these substances or these behaviors? Why?_____

_____

_____

12. What would be acceptable drinking behavior in our home? Check all that apply.

☐ beer   ☐ hard liquor   ☐ wine

☐ daily   ☐ once a week   ☐ several a week   ☐ several a month   ☐ on special occasions   ☐ never

13. Are either of us seeking professional help? If not, do I think that we should be?_____

_____

_____

14. How aware are we of the risk of AIDS infection from multiple sex partners and intravenous drug use? Have we discussed this? Why? Why not? _____

_____

_____

Note: This page is reproduced from the Couple's Book.

Her Page

Answer these questions by yourself. When you are finished discuss your answers and reflections with your partner.

1. Do I feel that you are trying to change me? How?_____
_____
_____
_____

2. How do I think that our personalities compliment each other?_____
_____
_____
_____

3. How do I feel about discussing my past relationships? Can I be honest? Do I think that you really listen to me and understand?_____
_____
_____

4. How do I feel about discussing your past relationships?_____
_____
_____

5. Am I concerned about my use of drugs or alcohol? spending habits? sexual activity? eating? or gambling?
_____
_____

6. Do I feel in control of these behaviors? Explain._____
_____
_____

7. When you are in a bad mood I usually…
    ☐ try to make you feel better   ☐ fix it   ☐ ignore you   ☐ feel bad
    ☐ offer to listen   ☐ give you your space

8. Do I think that I am responsible for your feelings?_____
_____
_____

9. Am I concerned about your use of drugs or alcohol? spending? sexual activity? eating? or gambling?
_____
_____
_____

31

Note: This page is reproduced from the Couple's Book.

10. Have I ever felt that any of these behaviors is out of control in your life? Explain._____

_____

_____

11. Do I feel that we need to discuss the use of these substances or these behaviors? Why?_____

_____

_____

12. What would be acceptable drinking behavior in our home? Check all that apply.

☐ beer   ☐ hard liquor   ☐ wine

☐ daily   ☐ once a week   ☐ several a week   ☐ several a month   ☐ on special occasions   ☐ never

13. Are either of us seeking professional help? If not, do I think that we should be?_____

_____

_____

14. How aware are we of the risk of AIDS infection from multiple sex partners and intravenous drug use? Have we discussed this? Why? Why not?_____

_____

_____

Note: This page is reproduced from the Couple's Book.

ISSUES OF SPECIAL FOCUS

If these issues pertain to you, discuss them with your partner.

1. Do I want you to meet or know my ex-spouse?

2. Am I able to share with you the "story" of my previous marriage, and the reason(s) for the breakup?

3. In what ways is the personality of my (our) children different from my personality? Your personality?

4. Are you aware of anyone in your family who has been mentally ill? Have you shared this with your partner?

RELATIONSHIP CHECK

Each of you should circle the number that best represents how you feel about your relationship after discussing this topic. Remember, you each need to select your own number.

      1. very close   2. somewhat close   3. somewhat distant   4. very distant

What do I want to discuss further with you?_____

_____

_____

_____

_____

_____

_____

_____

_____

DUAL-CAREER COUPLES

You've heard of "D.I.N.K." couples. D.I.N.K. stands for "dual income, no kids." Young, newly-married DINK couples are becoming the norm in our society today. It sounds great, doesn't it? Double the income, few restraints (like kids) . . . and a life of fast food, long hours at work, and a messy apartment or house awaiting you at the end of the day. You see, having two jobs is great, but it also demands of you an even higher level of communication and effort to make the several elements of your life work together.

If you will both work, ask yourselves the following questions: Who will clean the house? pay the bills? vacuum and mop? take the trash out? cut the grass? stay home for the repairmen? prepare the dinner? do dishes, laundry, grocery shopping? fix the leaky faucet? clean the bathtub, toilet, and bathroom?

Unfortunately, the traditional beliefs and behaviors of men and women in two-job marriages do not change just because both work outside the home. Studies show that women still do the majority of household chores regardless of the number of hours they spend at work. The entrenched perspective of the wife as homemaker still lingers in dual-career marriages. And the result could very well be a burned-out wife.

To help dual-career couples manage household chores, a graduate student at Southwest Texas State University developed a five-step approach. The following steps are intended to be done together.

STEP 1: Formulate a list of household chores.

STEP 2: Determine frequency of the tasks (daily, bi-weekly, etc.)

STEP 3: Agree on who is responsible to do the task: a) Consider each of your abilities and interests. b) Rotate the highly desirable or highly undesirable tasks.

STEP 4: Periodically review the chores to determine: a) Did the person designated do the task? b) Was it done to the satisfaction of both of you? c) If "no" is the answer to a or b, what prevented the completion of the chore? d) What more is needed (time, money, people) to get the chore done well?

STEP 5: Recycle: Add or drop chores, or change person responsible if necessary.

33

Note: This page is reproduced from the Couple's Book.

Two Different Directions

> Marriage is the joining of two unique individuals coming together from "two different directions." The challenge that every couple faces is how to blend these different directions to form one shared journey. True love is what it takes.

They say they love each other
I've no doubt they do
They say they'll always be together
That may not be true

They come from different places
Different points of view
They find themselves in different spaces
Everything is all brand new

Two different directions
Too many different ways
One always on the road somewhere
The other one always stays
Too often unhappy
Too often on your own
When you are moving in different directions
True love is all alone

Old stories start to surface
Patterns from long ago
And loving quickly turns to anger
For reasons they don't even know
The strongest heart can be broken
With one insensitive word
The deepest feelings remain unspoken
No one is seen and nothing heard

Note: This page is reproduced from the Couple's Book.

Two different directions
Too many different ways
One always wants to work things out
The other one wants to play
Too ready for changes
Too much that just can't wait
When you are moving in different directions
True love can turn to hate

If opposites attract each other
What's the reason for
One being like an open window
One just like a closing door

Two different directions
Too many different ways
One likes to see the morning sunrise
The other one sleeps in late
Too many tomorrows
Too many times too late
When you are moving in different directions
True love may have to wait
If you are committed to different directions
True love will have to wait.

—Lyrics by John Denver

35

Note: This page is reproduced from the Couple's Book.

Our Family of Origin

Family systems therapy is a rapidly growing field in mental health. Based upon systems theory, it examines the way an individual interacts within his or her family and environment. All of us are members of several systems at the same time. Although we each influence these systems, they in turn also influence each of us.

The most influential system in anyone's life is their family of origin. The "family system" acts like a machine, with numerous gears and cogs all rotating against each other. What affects one member, affects the whole system, and vice versa. This chapter helps the engaged individual look at his or her family of origin as a system of interrelating parts so that he or she will begin to notice the parts and how they fit together. The engaged couple will find these exercises fun and challenging.

Although there are several exercises in the couple's workbook, we are including one more here in the leader's edition. The Family Roadmap, as you can see, is not in the couple's edition.

Distribute copies of this exercise if time permits in your marriage preparation program schedule. It needs to be monitored though, and should not just be handed out for the couples to take home and do on their own. You'll need to make sure that there is paper for the couples to draw on and that each person has a copy of the Family Roadmap directions and model (this page is "photo-ready" in this volume).

With this exercise and all the exercises in this chapter, please heed the following warnings:

1. This is not therapy, and you are not therapists. Stress to the couples that the exercises in this chapter are for increased awareness and discovery. The results will undoubtedly be a renewed appreciation for certain parts of their upbringing, and a questioning of the value of certain other parts.

2. Avoid any hint of family bashing, that is, the tendency to lay blame for all problems on the family of origin. The point of this chapter is to start the individual looking to their family as a possible source of insights and/or answers for questions they may have about themselves. An individual or couple may choose later to pursue professional counseling to deal with past issues. However, be clear about your intention with this exercise: it is educative and not therapeutic!

3. Be alert for the individual or couple who may show signs of stress or negative emotional reaction to any of these exercises. They may need or want help. If this happens, your response should be to approach the individual or couple gently, during the break or after the session or program, and offer a referral to several recommended professional counselors, or to your diocesan Catholic social agency.

This is a delicate matter that needs to be evaluated and handled carefully, but it should be a team decision. As an individual team couple you may want to "rescue" an apparently hurting individual, but you may do more harm than good if you act alone. Talk to the other team members first and the priest/minister. Compare observations and recommendations. You may find that your observations are not supported by the other members. But if, as a team, you do decide that a particular individual or couple is upset or having problems, one of the team members should approach them at an appropriate time and offer counseling referrals. This approach should be gentle and quick. No "saving" or "rescuing," no "Lone Ranger" heroism. If the couple or individual wants professional counseling, it is their responsibility to get it.

The Family Roadmap: Directions and Model

A family roadmap, also known as a genogram, is like a family tree, except that it also includes how members relate to each other. A family roadmap is helpful in enabling an individual to see how his or her family of origin has developed and is developing. It gives a person a sense of one's roots. It is quite involved and will take a while to complete.

Using the symbols and the example on page 54, draw your family of origin roadmap. Start off by drawing either a square (for men) or a circle (for women) at the bottom of the page. Write your name below it and your age inside. Then proceed by working backward to any previous marriage or other serious relationship you've had; any children; your brothers or sisters; and finally to your parent(s). You may also choose to go a step beyond that and include your grandparents. Write down names, ages, and any brief, pertinent information next to each square or circle.

When you're done, place your roadmap next to your partners and draw a line between the woman's circle and the man's square. This combined family roadmap is now the roadmap that leads to your marriage! And it will be the family roadmap for any children you have.

The family roadmaps below, for Joe and Bev, reveal interesting relationships in their families of origin. You may want to discuss this imaginary couple's roadmap in your small group, or just refer to it as a model for doing your own family roadmap.

A Family Roadmap

Symbols:

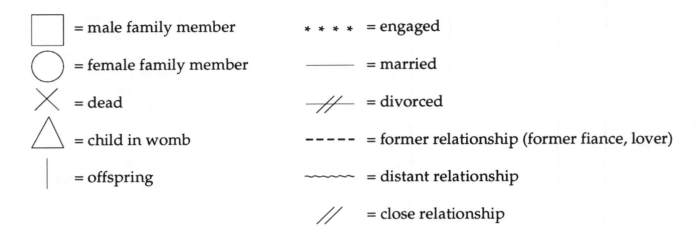

□ = male family member
○ = female family member
✕ = dead
△ = child in womb
| = offspring

* * * * = engaged
——— = married
—//— = divorced
----- = former relationship (former fiance, lover)
∼∼∼∼ = distant relationship
// = close relationship

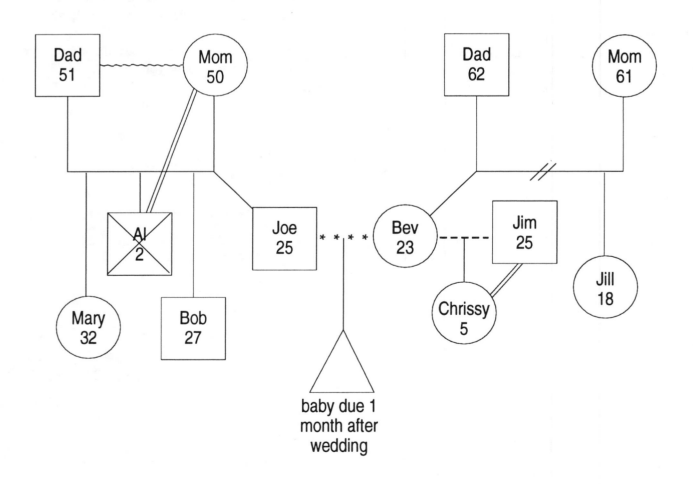

Notes

Chapter 4
Our Family of Origin

Carol cannot stand the way Ron chews his food. She accuses him of sounding like a cow.

Maria is totally bewildered by Hector's intense dislike of her holding onto his arm when they're in public.

Jonathan and Kate constantly argue over the proper place in the kitchen for the salt and pepper shakers–in the cabinet or on the table?

Tyrone is confused about why Leslie exploded and admonished him when he affectionately patted her on the bottom.

Bob cannot stand to receive any advice, from anybody, at any time. His wife, Pat, loves to seek out the suggestions of others.

Luis has no qualms about taking a few "leeways" in filling out their income tax form. Ida has a strict belief in always doing what is right, and thinks such a practice is dishonest.

Have you ever been at a loss to explain the seemingly peculiar actions, thoughts, feelings, behaviors, or likes/dislikes of your partner? Do you find yourself sometimes insisting on something because it's "common sense"?

Do you sometimes find yourself wondering why you behave or feel or think the way you do?

Many times our view of the world around us, our perceptions of our partner's actions and words, or even our consideration of what's "logical" or "normal" is the result of being raised in a particular family. Our family of origin influences each of us far more than we are usually aware.

Note: **This page is reproduced from the Couple's Book.**

Your feelings, your moods, your views of life, your sense of what is right and wrong, your internal sense of what's important and what isn't, all of this has been largely shaped by your family of origin. Even your idiosyncrasies may be the result of the home in which you were raised.

Poor Ron doesn't realize that the reason Carol accuses him of sounding like a cow when he chews his food is because she grew up sitting at the dinner table with her dad chewing his food with great gusto . . . and noise! Unfortunately, Carol also probably doesn't realize that that's the reason herself. All she knows is that she feels guilty and confused when she snaps at Ron.

Your family of origin is the family with whom you were raised. This may be a home with two, one, or no parents. It may include 12 siblings, or you as an only child. It may also have included grandparents. Whatever the make-up was, your family of origin is/was exactly what the name implies: the family from which you originated. The key players obviously are your parent(s). They were your first teachers, role models, and significant persons in your life.

For some people, the words "mom" and/or "dad" conjure up feelings of warmth, love, and care. For others, the feelings are anger and hurt. And for most people, there is a mixture of good and bad feelings associated with "mom" and "dad." Whatever your feelings are, one thing is for sure: these feelings and the experiences associated with them will affect your new marriage and new family!

Your "new" family is you and your partner and any children either of you may have. Once you are married, you are family. And the families from which each of you came become your families of origin.

A good way to visualize how your family of origin has influenced who you are today is to imagine that through all your years of growing up you were packing your suitcase for a long vacation away from mom and dad. The type of clothes you pack, what seems important to you to take on this long vacation, what seems unimportant, all represent the values, behaviors, thoughts, feelings, and idiosyncrasies that you bring to your marriage. We all bring our luggage full of old

---

LIVING WITH PARENTS

Back when our country was young, when folks tilled the fields, several generations of the same family lived together under one roof. With the Industrial Era, families of the 20th century became more fragmented. The American Dream was, and still is, to own your own house and move out of mom and dad's.

Today, many young couples find themselves moving back in with mom and dad. Financial restraints and saving to buy a house are the primary reasons for such a move. But what preparations are made in order for an easy and smooth adjustment for all concerned in such an arrangement?

Multi-generational homes are becoming more common. But surprisely few people in such arrangements plan ahead. Whether you're a young couple moving back in with parents, or you're an older couple with an elderly and/or infirmed parent moving in with you, a few simple tasks may help prevent hard feelings or stresses down the road.

1. Sit down and talk with your parents. What are their expectations of living with you? Express your desires.

2. Mutually establish some basic ground rules with the parents in regard to privacy, responsibilities, rights, and financial considerations.

3. Mutually establish a time line. If you are moving in with them, when will you be moving out?

4. After your wedding, sit down and discuss on a regular basis how the living arrangements are working out. What adjustments need to be made? What rules are working well? Which need to be changed?

5. Respect each other's "space"! Just because you live with mom and dad, don't assume they can drop everything just to pick you up at the service station.

Note: This page is reproduced from the Couple's Book.

family "stuff" to our marriages. And then often, sad to say, we spend the rest of our lives carrying that luggage around, guarding the contents as if it were priceless jewels, revealing only parts of it to our partners in defensive ways. We continuously seem to be amazed that we each have different "stuff" in our luggage, some of which is beautiful and worth keeping, and some of which is harmful and should be discarded.

We believe that it is important for each of you to sit down and open up your luggage now, and share the "stuff" inside, before you marry. The questions in this chapter will help you do that. There may be quite a few surprises, and it also may be a painful experience. Sharing who we truly are is never an easy task, even when it's with the one we love.

An important topic for each of you to look at and share is family of origin "rules." What were the "dos" and "don'ts" in the home in which you grew up? Some rules may be easy to remember because they were obvious rules, like "We all go to church every Sunday," or rules regarding homework or chores. Other rules, however, may have been more hidden or subconscious. These are the unspoken rules, like "We don't cry in this family," or "We don't show emotions," or "Don't hang your 'dirty laundry' out for the neighbors to see." The identification and naming of the parental rules under which you grew is important, because these rules, especially the hidden, unspoken ones, are the rules under which you probably still function today as an adult. And they may be harmful to your marriage and your own emotional well-being.

Think back to your childhood. What were the rules of the house? Focus on the unspoken rules, the ones which everyone knew but never talked about. This is hard to do, but nonetheless important. Usually the hidden rules of a family are based on how members should feel, think, behave, and cope with problems, and are typically "don't" rules.

Henry, the adult child of an alcoholic mother, was able to identify the "hidden rules" in his family. Very simply, they were: "You don't express feelings; You cope with problems by rationalizing them away; You always act as if life is great even when at home Mom is drinking." By naming these un-

Note: This page is reproduced from the Couple's Book.

spoken rules out loud, and then realizing how destructive they were to his own marriage, Henry was better able to deal with his wife, his children, and his own feelings.

These "hidden rules" of your family of origin have a life of their own. And, to return to the analogy of the vacation, they often sneak into your luggage without your knowing. You didn't consciously put them in, but they're there. And they are destructive!

In this chapter, you will find several exercises and questions that address the issue of family of origin. As with all the chapters in this workbook, you may not get to finish all the items contained here during your marriage preparation program. However, we strongly encourage you to finish all the exercises and questions in this chapter on your own, and to return to them throughout your marriage.

Your marriage is truly a journey. Know what "stuff" is in the luggage you're bringing with you!

A.C.O.A.

The phrase "Adult Children of Alcoholics" (A.C.O.A.), or simply "adult children," refers to the grown offspring of alcoholic parents who, as a result of being raised in a dysfunctional family, have acquired unhealthy feelings, traits, behaviors, values and/or thinking that ultimately takes away from their quality of life. ACOAs usually suffer from co-dependency (see information box on page 22). And, to make matters worse, ACOAs tend to marry alcoholics, addicts, or other ACOAs, thus perpetuating their own unhealthy co-dependency.

Often ACOAs are not fully aware of how destructive some of their behavior and thinking is. Deep down they know "something's not right," but they try to suppress what they're feeling in hopes that the "hurt" of growing up in an alcoholic home will go away. It won't. Not by itself.

If you or your partner grew up in a home where alcohol or drugs were regularly abused, chances are you're an ACOA. And if you are, you need a counselor to help you work through some of your feelings. It's not easy. But the alternative is worse: the alternative is an unhappy life.

See the Resource Appendix for information about national ACOA groups.

39

Note: This page is reproduced from the Couple's Book.

Dinner with the _____
Fill in your family name.

This exercise will require some time, quiet, and imagination. Whether you do this "imagery" exercise during a marriage preparation program or on your own, try to find some space by yourself to allow you to really get into it.

Visualize what a typical dinner time looked like in your family of origin when you were about 10 years old. Describe it to your partner by answering some or all of the following questions.

- Where is the dinner?
  (dining room? kitchen? in front of the TV? at a restaurant?)
- What are you eating?
- Who's present?
- Where does everyone sit in relation to one another?
- How do you, as a 10 year old, feel?

- Who's absent?
- Why are they absent?
- What's the topic(s) of conversation?
- Who does the talking?
- Who does the listening?
- What will each person do after dinner?

40

Note: This page is reproduced from the Couple's Book.

His Page

HOW "HEALTHY" WAS YOUR FAMILY OF ORIGIN?

In her 1983 *Traits of A Healthy Family*, Dolores Curran names 15 traits that "healthy families" have in common, chosen by 551 family health professionals, including priests, ministers, counselors, teachers, and social workers.

You will find these 15 traits of healthy families listed below. Read over each one and consider how it applies to your family of origin as you were growing up. For example, for the first trait ask yourself, "How well did my family of origin communicate and listen?" And then rate each trait by circling a number from 1 to 5. When you're done, draw a line connecting all your circles and go through your ratings with your partner, and discuss them.

A HEALTHY FAMILY...	MY FAMILY OF ORIGIN...			
	did not do this well	did this well sometimes		did this well
...communicates and listens.	1	2	3	4	5
...affirms and supports one another.	1	2	3	4	5
...teaches respect for others.	1	2	3	4	5
...develops a sense of trust.	1	2	3	4	5
...has a sense of play and humor.	1	2	3	4	5
...exhibits a sense of shared responsibility.	1	2	3	4	5
...teaches a sense of right and wrong.	1	2	3	4	5
...has a strong sense of family in which rituals and traditions abound.	1	2	3	4	5
...has a balance of interaction among members.	1	2	3	4	5
...has a shared religious core.	1	2	3	4	5
...respects the privacy of one another.	1	2	3	4	5
...values service to others.	1	2	3	4	5
...fosters family table time and conversation.	1	2	3	4	5
...shares leisure time.	1	2	3	4	5
...admits to and seeks help with problems.	1	2	3	4	5

41

Note: This page is reproduced from the Couple's Book.

Answer the following questions

1. What are three strengths in my family of origin?_____
_____
_____

2. What are three areas in which my family of origin was not strong?_____
_____
_____

3. What traits and/or idiosyncrasies do I see in you that I also see in your parent(s)?_____
_____
_____

4. How close was my family when I was growing up?

        1. very close   2. somewhat close   3. somewhat distant   4.very distant

Note: This page is reproduced from the Couple's Book.

Her Page

HOW "HEALTHY" WAS YOUR FAMILY OF ORIGIN?

In her 1983 *Traits of A Healthy Family*, Dolores Curran names 15 traits that "healthy families" have in common, chosen by 551 family health professionals, including priests, ministers, counselors, teachers, and social workers.

You will find these 15 traits of healthy families listed below. Read over each one and consider how it applies to your family of origin as you were growing up. For example, for the first trait ask yourself, "How well did my family of origin communicate and listen?" And then rate each trait by circling a number from 1 to 5. When you're done, draw a line connecting all your circles and go through your ratings with your partner, and discuss them.

A HEALTHY FAMILY...	MY FAMILY OF ORIGIN...			
	did not do this well	did this well sometimes		did this well
...communicates and listens.	1	2	3	4	5
...affirms and supports one another.	1	2	3	4	5
...teaches respect for others.	1	2	3	4	5
...develops a sense of trust.	1	2	3	4	5
...has a sense of play and humor.	1	2	3	4	5
...exhibits a sense of shared responsibility.	1	2	3	4	5
...teaches a sense of right and wrong.	1	2	3	4	5
...has a strong sense of family in which rituals and traditions abound.	1	2	3	4	5
...has a balance of interaction among members.	1	2	3	4	5
...has a shared religious core.	1	2	3	4	5
...respects the privacy of one another.	1	2	3	4	5
...values service to others.	1	2	3	4	5
...fosters family table time and conversation.	1	2	3	4	5
...shares leisure time.	1	2	3	4	5
...admits to and seeks help with problems.	1	2	3	4	5

43

Note: **This page is reproduced from the Couple's Book.**

Answer the following questions

1. What are three strengths in my family of origin?_____

_____

_____

2. What are three areas in which my family of origin was not strong?_____

_____

_____

3. What traits and/or idiosyncrasies do I see in you that I also see in your parent(s)?_____

_____

_____

4. How close was my family when I was growing up?

      1. very close   2. somewhat close   3. somewhat distant   4. very distant

Note: This page is reproduced from the Couple's Book.

ISSUES OF SPECIAL FOCUS

If these issues pertain to you, discuss them with your partner.

1. If one or both of you have children from a previous relationship, describe the family of origin of your child's other parent as best you can. Reflect on the questions and apply the exercises in this chapter.

2. If your parents have died, are there any unfinished, unsettled arguments or unspoken conversations that you wish you could have had, or completed with them? If so, write your parent(s) a letter and tell them what you would have wanted to say. Hold on to the letter and share it with your partner someday when you are ready.

3. If you were abused as a child, have you told your partner? Have you gone for counseling? If not, why?

GROUP SECTION

Discuss this case study as a group. Answer the following questions.
1. What do you think Maggie and Jeff need to look at regarding their families of origin?
2. What do each of them need to do?

CASE STUDY: MAGGIE AND JEFF

Maggie's eyes were filling with tears as she told the counselor of the problems she and Jeff were experiencing in their young marriage. Maggie likes to visit her parents often. They only live ten minutes away, and especially with her mother's recent illness, she feels a need to spend time with them.

Jeff doesn't like the idea that she's over there almost every day. The visits aren't always long, although she's been known to spend the entire evening there. It frustrates Jeff that she's always "running home to mommy and daddy."

Maggie was raised in a large, tight-knit family. She lived with her parents, whom she adored, right up to her marriage at the age of 23. Her father earned a good living and retired at an early age. Her mother was a dedicated, traditional wife and mother who managed the home well.

Jeff and his two younger brothers were raised by his father. His mother died when Jeff was nine. And although he gets along fine with this father, there is a "distance" there. Jeff's father had to be both mom and dad to his sons, which was difficult considering he held down two jobs most of this life. Jeff's strict paternal grandparents, who were from Germany, helped the father raise the boys. But

basically Jeff and his brothers grew up taking care of themselves. Their father was affectionate when he was home. And he was careful to tell the boys stories of their mother, lest they forget her.

Jeff looks at the counselor and says, "I don't know what's wrong with my wanting Maggie to spend less time with her parents and more time with me." Maggie, looking hurt, responds, "I am able to spend a little time with my folks and still have plenty of time for Jeff." The counselor recommends that they look at their families of origin to uncover some of their problems.

RELATIONSHIP CHECK

Each of you should circle the number that best represents how you feel about your relationship after discussing this topic. Remember, you each need to select your own number.

    1. very close   2. somewhat close   3. somewhat distant   4. very distant

What would I want to discuss further with you?_____

_____
_____
_____
_____
_____

45

Note: **This page is reproduced from the Couple's Book.**

Our Sexuality

The issues of sexuality and sex may be difficult for the engaged couple to address. Interestingly, in working with engaged couples we have found that there is often a mental chasm between what a couple thinks they know and what they really do know about sexuality. In other words, many couples think they pretty well know everything there is to know about sex and sexuality. This may be because their perspective is a more biological, action-focused one. Of course, as a team couple, you will not address the issue with the same perspective. The perspective of sexuality and sex revealed in this chapter focuses on personal relationships. A couple may feel that they are good at sex. But are they good at being well-rounded, loving sexual partners? There's a difference!

The engaged couples are presented with a who-listic perspective of sexuality and are challenged to look inside themselves for both the masculine and feminine traits in each of us. In presenting a talk on sexuality, you may want to consider taking our analogy of a diamond and elaborate on the many facets there are to the sexuality of a married couple. Nothing beats a good visual prop in a talk: bring in a large crystal dangling from a string and hold it up as you make the analogy.

Gender-specific roles is an important and lively issue these days. Are men to do only the "manly" jobs around the house? What about the "feminine" chores? Why the distinction? This whole topic is excellent for small group discussion, and will probably flow right out of the roles/traits exercise listed in the Group Section of the couple's edition.

The concluding paragraphs of this chapter look at sex as a beautiful, delicate gift from God. This perspective, held up against the backdrop of societal views of sex that often abuses it in advertising, entertainment, or money-making, is a refreshing alternative for most couples. We are all inundated with an endless flood of negative and unhealthy messages regarding sex, whether from television, magazines, movies, friends, the workplace, or school. This chapter holds out a powerful message for an engaged couple when they witness married couples who present sex as a God-given, holy form of communication between a husband and wife. It shatters the view of contemporary society.

Our Sexuality
Talk Outline

1. Introduce self and topic
- Number of years married?
- Any children? Ages?
- Town you live in? Church?
- How long involved as marriage preparation volunteer couple?
- Any other general information about yourselves?
- What's your topic?
- Why is it important for them, as engaged couples, to hear about this topic?

2. "Sexuality" is a word most of us equate with "sex"
- This is both unfortunate and incorrect.
- Actually sexuality refers to who you are as a person, and it includes your personality, beliefs, gender, feelings, behaviors, physical body, and ability to relate to others, to name a few.
- You are a sexual person, at *all* times, in *all* situations, not just when sex is involved.
- Sexuality involves how you feel about yourself—your self-image, self-esteem, and self-love.
- Feeling that you are unlovable and unattractive to your partner will adversely effect your marriage.

3. Feminine and masculine traits are in *each* of us
- Men will favor the masculine. Women will favor the feminine.
- The more you can balance the two, the healthier a person, and the better marriage partner you will be—and *the happier you'll be.*
- Traits of Feminine vs Masculine:

gentle	assertive
process-oriented	goal-oriented
feelings	thoughts
emotion	logic

- Both sets of traits are good. The important thing is balance between the two.

4. "Feminization" of marital relationship
- The traits listed as feminine are those that enhance the marital relationship.
- Those listed as masculine inhibit good communication and the sharing of self and feelings.
- The more feminine traits in your marriage and in your communication, the healthier your relationship.

5. Influences on our sexuality
- Family of Origin. Our parents defined for us as we were growing up what it meant to be a woman and a wife, by watching mom, and what it meant to be a man and a husband, by watching dad.
- Social pressures. Our society defines what it means to be a "real man" or a "real woman." Certain expectations are put upon us in order to be accepted in our culture.
- Media. Movies, advertisements, and other media define male and female behaviors. Whether we like it or not, they influence us.
- Church. Church teachings define Christian women and men, as well as sets up acceptable behaviors and manners of living.

6. As a Christian couple, we see our sexuality and sexual expression as good and as a gift from God

- Believe that our bodies are good, as able to comfort, care for and please each other.
- See intercourse as a special gift that strengthens our relationship, deepens our communication and intimacy, heals and comforts us, points to the fidelity of our marriage and the exclusiveness of our sexual expression.
- Our sexual expression offers us gifts and opportunities: to new life in our relationship, healing, renewing and nurturing our love, and to new life in the decision to have a child.

7. Having a child is a decision

- Demands honest communication about fears, feelings, and doubts.
- Need to discuss how many? when? finances? careers? day care? infertility? adoption? no children?

8. Need to challenge couples to keep their love life alive as they would any other form of communication

NOTES:

1. Read the couple's and leader's edition chapters on this topic.

2. Lace this and all talks with personal stories, examples, and anecdotes that add color and/or demonstrate what you are talking about.

Notes

Chapter 5
Our Sexuality

You may think, "Now comes the good part of the book...*sex!*" Well we hate to disappoint you, but the topic of this chapter is sexuality, and not just sex. While sexuality includes sex, it also includes much more.

Your sexuality is who you are as a person. It refers to you as a man or a woman. Now that you're engaged, this becomes more important than ever because you are going to have to help your partner understand what it means to live intimately with you. You probably think you know each other pretty well. But occasionally there will be things about each of you that will still surprise the other. No matter how long you have known each other or been married, there are still new things to discover about yourselves. And this only adds richness to your relationship.

Some of these new discoveries can be attributed to personality, some to education, some to how you were raised, and some just to your own likes and dislikes. But all of these surprises and unique little things are part of you as a sexual human being. Your sexuality permeates everything about you.

Such a holistic perspective should free you from some false assumptions and societal expectations. One such myth says that manhood or womanhood is linked to a person's ability to perform sex. This myth ignores the fact that you are a sexual person at all times, in all situations. Your masculinity and femininity is expressed in countless ways every day, and not only in bed.

As a sexual being, you are like a diamond. You're

Note: This page is reproduced from the Couple's Book.

one of a kind. You're beautiful and priceless to your partner. And, like a diamond, there are many facets to you as a sexual human being.

The first two facets of your sexuality are the feminine and masculine traits found in each of us. Men typically stress the masculine, and women the feminine. However, everyone needs to accept and use both masculine and feminine traits. In other words, women need to be in touch with and express their masculine side, and men their feminine side.

Some of the traits associated with our feminine side include nurturing, affection, compassion, sympathy, tenderness, understanding, gentleness, and an orientation toward feelings, people, and relationships. Those associated with the masculine side include protecting, ambition, dominance, self-reliance, forcefulness, aggression, and an orientation towards thoughts and things.

A healthy person embraces the traits from both. To be a complete and balanced person, it is necessary for women to be assertive and confident and for men to be tender and nurturing! Refusing to acknowledge these traits can cause problems in your relationship and hinder true communication. This sense of balance also extends into all areas of your relationship: your intimacy, role identification, and love making.

Another facet of your sexuality is intimacy, or the sharing of yourself with your partner in a focused, exclusive way. This is when we allow our partner to see who we really are, to share ourselves without defenses or pretenses. Intimacy is the glue that holds it all together. A lack of intimacy is often the cause of problems for a couple.

A couple came to see us complaining that the romance was gone. She was too tired and he too bored with the routine of their lovemaking so they just gave it up. When we talked about the other areas of their life—job, children, home life, we discovered they were so busy they didn't have time to talk to each other until 11:00 P.M. each night, at which time they tried to settle the day's activities with the kids, the bills, and their responsibilities to other family members. No wonder the romance was gone! After a few weeks of getting more

---

SEXUAL ADDICTION

Just as an alcoholic has a pathological addiction to alcohol, a sex addict has a pathological addiction to sex and unhealthy relationships. According to a 1989 brochure published by Golden Valley Health Center, Minneapolis, "Sexual addiction or dependency is defined as engaging in obsessive/ compulsive sexual behaviors which cause severe stress for the individual and his/her family. The addicted person is unable to control his/her behaviors and lives in constant fear of discovery."

Sexual addicts might engage in or use chronic masturbation, pornography, prostitution, might cultivate compulsive heterosexual or homosexual relationships, exhibitionism or voyeurism, might frequent "adult" book stores, might engage in anonymous sex, indecent phone calls, child molestation, incest, and rape. The addictive behavior becomes increasingly uncontrollable and ultimately destructive for the addict and those close to him/her.

Being a sex addict is more than being "a jock" or "a tease," and it's definitely not a joke. For more information, see the resource appendix at the end of this workbook.

47

Note: This page is reproduced from the Couple's Book.

time together to focus on their relationship and settling the big family issues earlier in the day, they discovered that their sex life wasn't really gone after all. Intimacy in their communication renewed the intimacy in their love making.

But how do you become intimate in your communication? It strikes us that men and women do communicate differently about close interpersonal relations, as the following lists show:

Qualities of Female Communication	Qualities of Male Communication
Focus on the process	Focus on the results
Sensitive, feeling	Keep to the facts
Sharing	Logical
Confront and settle issues	Avoid issues
Give and take	Who's right?
Express	Suppress
Assertive	Aggressive
Compassionate	Analytical
Gentle	Dominant

Although each approach to communication has its merits and deficiencies, the female qualities listed above tend to improve intimacy in couple communication better than do the male qualities. This feminization of marital communication, when talking with the one you love, invites us to be sensitive, sharing, expressive, compassionate, and gentle. This, of course, is not a hard, fast rule. There are times when you need to stick to the facts, reach a conclusion quickly, and be logical. But generally speaking, the more *gentle* you can be with each other, the more intimate your communication will be.

Another facet of your sexuality as husband and wife will include role identification and who will do what around the house. Traditionally, household chores have been gender-specific. Wives do certain jobs because these jobs are considered feminine, and husbands perform the masculine jobs. However, over the past thirty years there has emerged a more egalitarian approach toward household tasks. In such a model, the couple looks at each of their individual strengths, likes, and dislikes, and then mutually decides who should do what. We recommend that you follow such an egalitarian ap-

INFERTILITY

The U.S. Public Health Service estimates that approximately 25 percent of married couples experience long-term fertility problems. They cannot conceive a child at all, or they cannot have as many as they'd like.

Infertility is not an uncommon problem for couples. And yet when a couple experiences difficulty or inability to conceive a child, they often feel isolated and alone. "Everyone else can have a baby, why can't we?"

Infertility may be connected to male impotence, low sperm count, sterility or defective sperm or egg production as the result of infectious diseases, blocked Fallopian tubes, or various other reasons.

Fertility should not be perceived in relation to manhood or womanhood. But unfortunately this false connection is made, especially by men. Virility and fertility are seen as synonymous. Fertility problems are not connected to how much of a man or woman you are. Fertility problems are not rare. And fertility problems should not be kept a secret or kept in the dark. The more you seek professional advice, and confide in trusted friends or family, the more you'll realize how common it is.

Consult a physician if you think you are infertile. There are a variety of methods of treatment that work well.

48

Note: This page is reproduced from the Couple's Book.

proach in divvying up household chores. It further enhances couple communication and ultimately provides the most satisfaction to each of you.

When we moved to a new house several years ago, it was a common sight every Saturday morning to see husbands out cutting the grass. However, because of work and school responsibilities, John wasn't able to do much of the grass mowing. Consequently, Sue was typically out there every weekend, cutting the grass with all the husbands. After several weeks of humorous little comments from the neighbors regarding our nontraditional ways, we noticed that some of the other women started cutting the grass. By the end of the summer, it was mostly the women pushing the mowers every weekend. Where were the men? We were almost afraid to ask, but we hope they were inside doing the laundry or changing the baby!

The final facet of your sexuality is sex. Physical sharing of yourself with your partner is one of the most intimate forms of communication in your relationship. It is here that you give yourself to your partner physically, emotionally, psychologically, and spiritually. And it is in the giving and receiving of each other that love-making can be mutually life-giving and satisfying.

Sex is a gift given by a good God to a loving couple. It possesses, beyond all other communications, the unique power to create new life in the couple's relationship as well as in the form of a child. It is here in its potential to create that we are privileged to glimpse the handiwork of God in our relationships.

Most of us have been influenced by the ideas that sex and God were separate and that somehow sex or things of the body were shameful. We have also witnessed a society that flaunts and abuses sex and the body through pornography and promiscuity. While these ideas about sex may have influenced us, we need not accept them.

Our love making and sexuality are gifts to us from a loving Creater, to be nurtured lovingly. Handle them gently and your marriage will grow and blossom.

A.I.D.S.

As of December, 1991, there were a total of 206,392 cases of AIDS reported to U.S. public health officials. Of those, 133,233 had died. This is close to double the number of Americans dead from the Vietnam War. Of the reported cases, 60% are gay men, 30% are intravenous drug abusers, 7% are patients with blood-clotting disorders requiring frequent blood transfusions, and 2% are the result of heterosexual sex.

Dr. James Curran, director of the AIDS program at the U.S. Center for Disease Control, predicts over 500,000 more reported cases by the year 2000.

Clearly, homosexual males and IV drug users are the largest at-risk populations. But this does not imply that the average married couple, who does not use intravenous drugs, will be left unscathed by this scourge. The 2% reported cases of heterosexual victims may appear low. But some simple math, and some foresight about what the numbers will be by the year 2000, points to the fact that this is a disease that is everyone's concern. AIDS does not discriminate. Soon there will be no one who at least doesn't know someone who is HIV-positive.

Your chances of acquiring the AIDS virus, if you do not fit into the categories of gay men, IV drug abusers, or recipient of frequent blood transfusions, are low. However, you and your marriage *will* be affected by AIDS—whether it be a family member, friend, co-worker, or neighbor. The more you can educate yourself, the better. AIDS is a reality which we all need to be informed about.

See the Resource Appendix at the end of the book for information on national A.I.D.S. organizations.

Note: This page is reproduced from the Couple's Book.

NATURAL FAMILY PLANNING

Natural Family Planning (NFP) refers to several methods of avoiding or achieving pregnancy that cooperate with a couple's own natural fertility. Unlike artificial birth control, which suppresses a couples' natural fertility by means of drugs or contraceptive devices, NFP is 100 percent natural.

Natural Family Planning is not to be confused with the old calendar "rhythm" method, which often proved to be unreliable. Unlike rhythm, which simply used mathematical calendar calculations to predict ovulation, NFP is based on the observation of the fertile and infertile periods of a woman's cycle. Couples abstain from intercourse during the fertile phase of the cycle if they are using NFP to avoid pregnancy. For couples who are finding it difficult to conceive a child, NFP is helpful in its emphasis on fertility awareness.

In several studies, including the 1978 five-country study by the World Health Organization, NFP was found to be 97-99 percent effective, equal to the pill, but more effective than the I.U.D. and the condom.

Natural Family Planning is morally acceptable to all religions, and is in harmony with the official teaching of the Catholic church, which prohibits any means of artificial contraception.

There are two commonly used NFP methods: the Ovulation Method and the Sympto-Thermal Method. Both are very reliable and effective. Instruction by a qualified instructor is essential with NFP. Contact your church or diocese to find out more information and when classes are held.

For more information, we recommend the following publications:

Family Planning: A Guide for Exploring the Options, Charles and Elizabeth Balsam (Liguori, Mo.: Liguori Publications, 1985)

No-Pill, No-Risk Birth Control, Nona Aguilar (Rawson Wade Publishers, 1980)

The Art of Natural Family Planning, John and Sheila Kippley (Couple to Couple League, 1984)

Challenge to Love, Mary Shivanandan (KM Associates, 1979).

Note: This page is reproduced from the Couple's Book.

His Page

1. How comfortable am I in discussing sex with you? (Circle one.)
How comfortable are you? (Put an X on one.)

    1. very uncomfortable   2. somewhat uncomfortable   3. somewhat comfortable   4. very comfortable

2. On a scale if 1 to 5 (5=highest), how affectionate do I think you are? (Circle one.)
How affectionate do I wish you would be? (Put an X on one.)

        1   2   3   4   5

3. What do I find most physically attractive about you?_____

4. What do I think is my most physically attractive feature?_____

5. In my family of origin: sex was... (check as many as appropriate)

    ☐ never discussed   ☐ viewed as a gift from God   ☐ openly talked about

    ☐ the focus of many jokes   ☐ considered "dirty"   ☐ other_____

6. True or False:

	T	F	
	☐	☐	To me, sex is extremely important.
	☐	☐	To you, sex is extremely important.
	☐	☐	Once we are married, I have a right to your body.
	☐	☐	If I'm angry at you, I have a right to withhold sex.
	☐	☐	Romance comes naturally.
	☐	☐	If you cheated on me I would end our marriage.

7. Once we are married, do I think that I will be able to initiate our lovemaking, or will I wait until you do?

_____

8. Will I be able to say "no"? How will I feel if you say "no"?

_____

_____

9. If I was sexually abused or raped, have I talked with you about it? Have I sought counseling?

_____

10. Have we discussed any past sexual relationships? Did the discussion effect our relationship? How?

_____

_____

11. Am I aware of the risk of AIDS from sex? Are you?

_____

                                                                           51

Note: This page is reproduced from the Couple's Book.

12. Have I ever been tested for the AIDS virus? Have you?

_____

Have we discussed this? Is this something that I think that we need to talk more about?

_____

13. How do I feel about sex outside of marriage?

_____

_____

14. Are there any sexual acts within marriage that I will find unacceptable? What?

_____

_____

15. In our everyday dealings with each other,
I wish you would be:

☐ ☐ more gentle
☐ ☐ stronger
☐ ☐ more expressive with your emotions
☐ ☐ more independent
☐ ☐ more caring
☐ ☐ more open with your thoughts
☐ ☐ less emotional
☐ ☐ less hesitant to make decisions
☐ ☐ more attentive to my needs
☐ ☐ less demanding
☐ ☐ more willing to negotiate

16. Have we talked about family planning and birth control? What have we decided? Who made the decision?_____

_____

17. Have I ever participated in any of the following behaviors? Have you? (Check those that apply.)

☐ vouyerism (peeping tom)   ☐ adult book stores
☐ exhibitionism   ☐ pedophilia (sex with children)
☐ anonymous sex (sex with strangers) ☐ incestuous relations
☐ prostitution (sex for pay)   ☐ massage parlors

18. If our sex life was in trouble, would I want us to seek counseling? Do I think that you would agree to it?_____

19. Is there anything about sex that I want to ask or talk about with someone other than you?

_____

52

Note: This page is reproduced from the Couple's Book.

Her Page

1. How comfortable am I in discussing sex with you? (Circle one.)
How comfortable are you? (Put an X on one.)

    1. very uncomfortable   2. somewhat uncomfortable   3. somewhat comfortable   4.very comfortable

2. On a scale if 1 to 5 (5=highest), how affectionate do I think that you are? (Circle one.)
How affectionate do I wish you would be? (Put an X on one.)
        1   2   3   4   5

3. What do I find most physically attractive about you?_____

4. What do I think is my most physically attractive feature?_____

5. In my family of origin: sex was... (check as many as appropriate)
    ☐ never discussed   ☐ viewed as a gift from God   ☐ openly talked about
      ☐ the focus of many jokes   ☐ considered "dirty"   ☐ other_____

6. True or False: T   F

                    ☐ ☐ To me, sex is extremely important.
                    ☐ ☐ To you, sex is extremely important.
                    ☐ ☐ Once we are married, I have a right to your body.
                    ☐ ☐ If I'm angry at you, I have a right to withhold sex.
                    ☐ ☐ Romance comes naturally.
                    ☐ ☐ If you cheated on me I would end our marriage.

7. Once we are married, do I think that I will be able to initiate our lovemaking, or will I wait until you do?

_____

8. Will I be able to say "no"? How will I feel if you say "no"?

_____
_____

9. If I was sexually abused or raped, have I talked with you about it? Have I sought counseling?

_____

10. Have we discussed any past sexual relationships? Did the discussion effect our relationship? How?

_____
_____

11. Am I aware of the risk of AIDS from sex? Are you?

_____

53

Note: This page is reproduced from the Couple's Book.

12. Have I ever been tested for the AIDS virus? Have you?

_____

Have we discussed this? Is this something that I think that we need to talk more about?

_____

13. How do I feel about sex outside of marriage?

_____

_____

14. Are there any sexual acts within marriage that I will find unacceptable? What?

_____

_____

15. In our everyday dealings
with each other, I wish you would be: ☐ ☐ more gentle
                                             ☐ ☐ stronger
                                             ☐ ☐ more expressive with your emotions
                                             ☐ ☐ more independent
                                             ☐ ☐ more caring
                                             ☐ ☐ more open with your thoughts
                                             ☐ ☐ less emotional
                                             ☐ ☐ less hesitant to make decisions
                                             ☐ ☐ more attentive to my needs
                                             ☐ ☐ less demanding
                                             ☐ ☐ more willing to negotiate

16. Have we talked about family planning and birth control? What have we decided? Who made the decision?_____

_____

17. Have I ever participated in any of the following behaviors? Have you? (Check those that apply.)

☐ vouyerism (peeping tom)   ☐ adult book stores
☐ exhibitionism   ☐ pedophilia (sex with children)
☐ anonymous sex (sex with strangers)   ☐ incestuous relations
☐ prostitution (sex for pay)   ☐ massage parlors

18. If our sex life was in trouble, would I want us to seek counseling? Do I think that you would agree to it?_____

19. Is there anything about sex that I want to ask or talk about with someone other than you?

_____

<u>54</u>

Note: This page is reproduced from the Couple's Book.

GROUP SECTION

Answer the following questions as a couple and then discuss your answers with other couples.

1. Which roles or traits listed below do you, as a couple, believe should be associated with men, women, or both? (Mark with an M for Men. Mark with a W for Women. Mark with a B for Both.)

☐ dominant	☐ writes letters	☐ dependent	☐ cooks
☐ protective	☐ homemaker	☐ expressive	☐ active
☐ aggressive	☐ works full-time	☐ distant	☐ emotional
☐ soft spoken	☐ plans vacations	☐ cuts grass	☐ strong
☐ nurturing	☐ does grocery shopping	☐ loud	☐ weak
☐ precise	☐ takes garbage out	☐ healer	☐ breadwinner
☐ provider	☐ changes diapers	☐ gentle	☐ cleans
☐ patient	☐ creative	☐ independent	☐ does banking
☐ compassionate	☐ pays bills	☐ passive	☐ does laundry
☐ works part-time	☐ loving	☐ works on cars	☐ vacuums
☐ disciplines kids	☐ leader	☐ does dishes	☐ follower

2. If you were to explain sexuality and sex to your child, what would you want them to know? Why? What would you not tell him or her?

ISSUES OF SPECIAL FOCUS

If these issues pertain to you, discuss them with your partner.

1. As a couple with a great age difference, how will our sex life be affected in the years to come?

2. How will our children from past relationships affect our sex life? Family planning? Privacy?

RELATIONSHIP CHECK

Each of you should circle the number that best represents how you feel about your relationship after discussing this topic. Remember, you each need to select your own number.

1. very close   2. somewhat close   3. somewhat distant   4. very distant

What would I want to discuss further with you?

_____
_____
_____

55

Note: This page is reproduced from the Couple's Book.

Chapter 6

Our Children

"Do you want to have children?"

"Oh yes, we'd love to have a baby!"

"No, I asked whether you want to have children. They're only babies for a short time. But they'll be your children all your life."

This conversation between an older married couple and a young engaged couple continued with a discussion about the responsibilities and hardships, and the joys and thrills involved in raising children. The engaged couple quickly caught on: deciding whether to have children, when, and how many is a life-altering decision. It's not a difficult concept to understand and yet many young couples without children do not realize it unless it's pointed out to them.

Young couples who are expecting or planning to have a child will usually plan the nursery well, buy all the necessary blankets, clothes, toys, and maybe even look ahead to start a college fund. However, few young couples are prepared for the day-to-day challenges of being a parent. "Once you're a parent, you're always a parent!"

One big turn-off for young couples is an older couple who smiles that all-knowing smile, and enunciates little pearls of wisdom such as, "Just you wait and see!" or "Oh my God, wait until you have children!" or "Enjoy yourselves now, 'cause once you have children...." Please don't speak to a young couple in that vein. It's better to speak of the love, satisfaction, and joy involved in watching children grow than of the personal hardships and difficulties you have had in raising them. We typically say something like, "We absolutely love being a mother and father....But having children has changed our lives very much." The engaged couple usually gets the picture.

An engaged couple should discuss in detail the timing and number of children. If you encounter a couple who hasn't talked about it at all or who seem to think having children is "no big deal," talk to them earnestly! Don't give them any pearls of wisdom—just speak from the heart.

Notes

Chapter 6
Our Children

At a recent marriage preparation program, an engaged couple approached us during one of the refreshment breaks. Our topic was children and parenting, and some of what we said had obviously struck a nerve with this couple. They were an attractive, intelligent couple in love, but they had a major problem. They explained that they were to be married in two months, and that they disagreed on the issue of children. He wanted one, possibly two, in four or five years. She wanted a lot of children, and wanted to start right away. They had discussed it at length, and were still unable to resolve the issue. We tried to put their dilemma into some perspective.

Several years ago, Sue was counseling a married couple in their early 40s. Their problem as they presented it was their sexual relationship. However, after several sessions, the real problem surfaced. They had been married for 15 years and had never settled their dilemma regarding children. Like the engaged couple above, this couple had disagreed on the number and timing of children. They hadn't addressed the issue in detail before they married. And after their wedding, the issue became so heated that their marriage almost ended in divorce after only one year. The fact that they had only one child was not the result of an agreed upon family plan. Rather, because of the unresolved issue, they rarely made love.

We had no simple answer for that engaged couple at the marriage preparation program. But we did emphasize that they had to resolve the problem before they married. And the answer had to be one that they

Note: **This page is reproduced from the Couple's Book.**

each agreed to and could live with, without resentment.

You and your partner must also address, in detail, the number and timing of children before you begin your marriage. If one or both of you have children already, do not assume that you agree on the prospects of having a child together in the future.

We waited four years before we had our first child. We had discussed this at length before our wedding and had come to an agreement. Interestingly enough, we changed our minds after we married but still were in agreement. It was as if our initial groundwork in communicating on family planning had given us the right tools to continually dialogue and revise our plans along the way.

The night before Justin was born, we were sitting on the floor in the newly-painted nursery reflecting upon our first four years of marriage, and wondering what it would be like to no longer be a twosome. With some sadness we realized that our lives were about to change dramatically. We felt a sense of hope and a sense of loss. We knew that one stage of our relationship was about to end, and a new one to begin. We had an overwhelming sense of "passage," as if we were about to walk through a one-way door. Looking back we're amazed at how accurate our feelings were. Having a child is definitely a one-way passage. After this, your life is never the same.

Just as it takes two of you to conceive a child, it takes two of you to raise a child. Mothers as well as fathers need to take responsibility for the nurturing, loving, and disciplining. For your children's sake, each of you has to supply plenty of time together, hugs, kisses, and appropriate discipline. And please notice we use the term "discipline" and not "punishment." Discipline, which comes from the same word as disciple, refers to educating and guiding your child. Punishment is negative, abusive, and counterproductive to raising a healthy, loving child.

Consider how you were raised. If you were abused physically, sexually, emotionally, or spiritually, you will have a greater tendency to similarly mistreat your offspring. If you were an abused child, we strongly recommend that you seek professional counseling. Seeing a counselor is a sign of health

---

AND BABY MAKES...?

In spite of the fact that more couples today are choosing to remain childless, the overall expectation of society is that a young couple will eventually, if not right away, have children. Having children is expected. It's seen as the norm. Often the phrase "starting a family" is used. This is unfortunate because you started your family the day you married. A childless couple is a family.

But, will you have children? What are your reasons? If any of the following reasons seem good to you, then think again!

1. "My (our) parents would die if we didn't."

2. "Why not? All my friends are having babies."

3. "Babies are so cute...I want one!"

4. "Having a baby will strengthen (save) our marriage."

5. "It's sort of expected; besides, it won't change our relationship that much."

6. "I want to stay home and not work."

7. "I want a baby to give me an identity. To make me feel important."

The following are some good reasons for wanting a child.

1. "As mature adults, we are deciding to have a baby and to assume all the responsibilities associated with it."

2. "Our relationship is sound and our love is secure; we want to raise a child in our warm, nurturing home."

3. "We are looking forward to rearing a child from birth to adulthood."

4. "We have so much love to give."

5. "I am psychologically and emotionally mature enough to be a parent to a baby who will be totally dependent on me."

The effect children have on marriage is tremendous! A baby can bring unbelievable joy, and frustration, to a couple. Parenting is an experience of both agony and ecstasy... ask any parent!

57

Note: This page is reproduced from the Couple's Book.

and is the mature thing to do for yourself, your spouse, and your children.

As an engaged couple, what should you consider in your discussion about having and raising children? Part of that discussion should include the impact that the birth of a child will have on your job(s) and, more importantly, how your jobs may affect your children. Too often, one partner assumes that the other will stop working, put a career on hold, and stay home with the baby. Assuming rather than talking it out usually develops into a problem.

Explore your options, be honest with each other, and make your decision together. You may want to start off by discussing your responses to the following: Which of us wants to stay home? Which of us wants to work outside the home? Is part-time work an option? What child care options do we have? What do I feel is best for our children? Remember too that the decision you make as a couple can be adapted and changed as time goes by and the number or ages of the children change.

Acknowledge, too, that just because you're biologically equipped to produce a child does not mean you are emotionally, spiritually, and developmentally ready to be a mom or a dad. Being a good parent requires neither a Ph.D. in child psychology nor memorization of one of the many child-care books on the market. It does require some more basic things: maturity, a capacity to love and to be loved, a commitment to your marriage and to your children. Bringing a child into the world is a decision that you as a couple should make together. Some couples will decide to wait, while others may decide to have a child early in their marriage. And still other couples may decide for very good reasons not to bring a child into the world at all.

Finally, being a good parent embraces a sense of "the spiritual" in all life. A child is not just flesh and bones, but a person, separate from its mother and father. Each child is a unique creation of God, an awesome symbol that life and love should continue. In the process of bringing new life into the world, we enter into the realm of the divine. We become co-creators with God, a role that should not be taken lightly.

MISCARRIAGES & STILLBIRTHS

For those women and couples who experience a miscarriage or a stillbirth, the sense of loss and sorrow can range from mild to devastating. Approximately one of four pregnancies will result in miscarriage or stillbirth. Women over 35, and those who smoke, drink alcohol, or do drugs are more likely to miscarry. After twenty weeks of pregnancy the spontaneous natural termination of the fetus' life is referred to as a stillbirth, and no longer technically as a miscarriage.

But more important than these facts on miscarriage and stillbirth are the feelings associated. For some reason, in the general consciousness of society there is a lack of understanding and empathy for those who have experienced such a loss. People tend to minimize it. Family and friends have been know to make idiotic and heartless statements such as: "Don't worry, you can try again," or "Who are we to question God's plans?"

For those who have experienced a miscarriage or stillbirth, especially couples who are trying to have a child, the grieving for the unborn baby is very real and very normal. The prospects of having another child are no consolation at the time. And family and friends can help the most by offering the couple a shoulder to cry on, an ear to listen, and a hand to hold.

58

Note: This page is reproduced from the Couple's Book.

His Page

1. How many children do I want?_____

2. How long do I want to wait until we have a baby?_____

3. Do I think I would be/am a good parent? Explain:_____
_____

4. As a parent, I will emphasize and/or supply the following for our children.
(Pick 4 and number in order, 1 = highest priority):

☐ college fund(s)   ☐ plenty of hugs & kisses   ☐ a love of life   ☐ good education

☐ a sense of right & wrong ☐ church attendance   ☐ discipline   ☐ whatever they want

☐ self-respect   ☐ love of God   ☐ the latest clothes   ☐ fear of God

☐ respect for others   ☐ respect for environment   ☐ toys   ☐ lots of fun times

5. I think having children will change/impact our marriage (Circle):   1. not at all   2. some   3. significantly

6. What's my main reason for wanting a child?_____
_____

7. How would I respond if our baby was born with physical or mental problems?_____
_____
_____

8. True or False:

T   F   T   F

☐ ☐ We both have to discipline our children.   ☐ ☐ Family planning is the woman's responsibility.

☐ ☐ Having a baby can help a marriage in trouble.   ☐ ☐ Children are a gift from God.

☐ ☐ Our children will have to adapt to our lifestyle. ☐ ☐ In an unwanted pregnancy, I'd consider abortion.

☐ ☐ Spanking is good for a child.   ☐ ☐ Our children will probably be put in day care.

☐ ☐ Our baby will always be the center of our lives.   ☐ ☐ It's primarily up to the mother.

☐ ☐ Feeling loved is probably one of the greatest gifts.

9. Have we talked about family planning? What method of family planning/birth control do I foresee us using?
_____
_____

59

Note: **This page is reproduced from the Couple's Book.**

10. Who will be the primary care provider for our children during the day? Me? You? Grandparents? Neighbor/Friend? Day-care center? other? _____

_____

11. What effect will having a baby have on our income? And our jobs? _____

_____

_____

12. If I had a choice between maintaining a certain level of income and lifestyle by keeping my job, or quitting my job so that I can stay home with our children, what would I choose? _____

_____

_____

JEALOUSY

Love and jealousy are not the same. As Margaret Mead (1968) stated, "Jealousy is not a barometer by which the depth of love can be read. It merely records the degree of the lover's insecurity . . . It is a negative, miserable state of feeling having its origin in the sense of insecurity and inferiority."

We are all jealous at one time or another. But if it becomes an ongoing experience, there may be a problem. Continuing suspicious feelings about a partner's fidelity tend to create further suspicions. An irrational preoccupation with keeping watch on your partner is destructive.

Ongoing jealousy is based on a poor self-image. And it is also difficult to hide from others. Unfortunately, some individuals will actually attempt to make their partner jealous in order to test the relationship, get attention, or "get back at" him or her for some perceived crime.

What do you do if jealousy is a recurring presence in your relationship? Sit down and talk it out! Is one of you intentionally making the other jealous? Why? What makes one of you jealous? What can you do as a couple to alleviate the problem? And finally, if you are the jealous person, you may want to scrutinize your own level of security. If you have recurring strong feelings of jealousy, you may want to talk to a professional counselor.

60

Note: This page is reproduced from the Couple's Book.

Her Page

1. How many children do I want?_____

2. How long do I want to wait until we have a baby?_____

3. Do I think I would be/am a good parent? Explain:_____
_____

4. As a parent, I will emphasize and/or supply the following for our children.
(Pick 4 and number in order, 1 = highest priority):

☐ college fund(s)   ☐ plenty of hugs & kisses   ☐ a love of life   ☐ good education

☐ a sense of right & wrong ☐ church attendance   ☐ discipline   ☐ whatever they want

☐ self-respect   ☐ love of God   ☐ the latest clothes   ☐ fear of God

☐ respect for others   ☐ respect for environment   ☐ toys   ☐ lots of fun times

5. I think having children will change/impact our marriage (Circle):   1. not at all   2. some   3. significantly

6. What's my main reason for wanting a child?_____
_____

7. How would I respond if our baby was born with physical or mental problems?_____
_____
_____

8. True or False:

T   F   T   F

☐ ☐ We both have to discipline our children.   ☐ ☐ Family planning is the woman's responsibility.

☐ ☐ Having a baby can help a marriage in trouble.   ☐ ☐ Children are a gift from God.

☐ ☐ Our children will have to adapt to our lifestyle.   ☐ ☐ In an unwanted pregnancy, I'd consider abortion.

☐ ☐ Spanking is good for a child.   ☐ ☐ Our children will probably be put in day care.

☐ ☐ Our baby will always be the center of our lives.   ☐ ☐ It's primarily up to the mother.

☐ ☐ Feeling loved is probably one of the greatest gifts.

9. Have we talked about family planning? What method of family planning/birth control do I foresee us using?
_____
_____

61

Note: This page is reproduced from the Couple's Book.

10. Who will be the primary care provider for our children during the day? Me? You? Grandparents? Neighbor/Friend? Day-care center? other? _____

_____

11. What effect will having a baby have on our income? And our jobs? _____

_____

_____

12. If I had a choice between maintaining a certain level of income and lifestyle by keeping my job, or quitting my job so that I can stay home with our children, what would I choose?_____

_____

_____

JEALOUSY

Love and jealousy are not the same. As Margaret Mead (1968) stated, "Jealousy is not a barometer by which the depth of love can be read. It merely records the degree of the lover's insecurity . . . It is a negative, miserable state of feeling having its origin in the sense of insecurity and inferiority."

We are all jealous at one time or another. But if it becomes an ongoing experience, there may be a problem. Continuing suspicious feelings about a partner's fidelity tend to create further suspicions. An irrational preoccupation with keeping watch on your partner is destructive.

Ongoing jealousy is based on a poor self-image. And it is also difficult to hide from others. Unfortunately, some individuals will actually attempt to make their partner jealous in order to test the relationship, get attention, or "get back at" him or her for some perceived crime.

What do you do if jealousy is a recurring presence in your relationship? Sit down and talk it out! Is one of you intentionally making the other jealous? Why? What makes one of you jealous? What can you do as a couple to alleviate the problem? And finally, if you are the jealous person, you may want to scrutinize your own level of security. If you have recurring strong feelings of jealousy, you may want to talk to a professional counselor.

62

Note: This page is reproduced from the Couple's Book.

GROUP SECTION

"BABY" CASES: Discuss these case studies as a group, answering the questions at the end of each.

GINNY & WIL: Ginny and Wil waited 7 years before they attempted to have a child. They're now in their mid-30's and have found that they are not able to have children. The resulting stress and anxiety has made them lash out at each other. They feel that their marriage may end. What do you think they need to do?

BOB & NICKI: Since they brought her home from the hospital, Bob and Nicki's cute little bundle of joy has turned into a big bundle of "terror." Little Heather is colicky. She cries and screams throughout the night, every night. No one sleeps. The doctor says there's nothing they can do except "wait it out." But after very little sleep over several weeks, Bob is starting to be late at work and Nicki is depressed and moody. What further problems may develop? What can they do? Make a list of suggestions.

JEFF & ANN: Jeff and Ann have a strong marriage based on good communication skills. However, since they had Nathaniel, they find they're not communicating as well. Ann is angry that Jeff does not get more involved in caring for Nathaniel; Jeff is angry because of their sudden loss of freedom. And when they try to talk about their feelings, little Nathaniel cries, needs to be changed or fed. What can they do to improve their situation?

MARY & LYLE: Lyle works at a factory and earns significantly less money than his wife, Mary, does as an executive secretary. They're planning on having a baby. And they agree that they don't want to put the baby in daycare. Someone will have to stay home. But it would be difficult for them to live on Lyle's income alone. And yet, he feels strongly that he should continue working. After several fights on the subject, Mary's wondering if they'll ever have a baby at all! They've decided to see a marriage counselor. What do you think the marriage counselor will have them focus on? How would you handle the situation?

YOUNG AND PREGNANT BEFORE THE WEDDING

We often think teenagers and young people in their early twenties feel indestructible. Even when they see their own friends die from drinking and driving, or become pregnant, or messed up with drugs, they often intuitively believe, "It can't happen to me."

Counselors refer to this feeling of indestructibility as a personal fable. In other words, it encompasses the false, unrealistic view about self that allows a young person to take risks.

People who become pregnant by accident are usually very aware of the risk of sexual intercourse, and yet still get pregnant. Why? They didn't think it could happen to them.

And yet, once they get pregnant, many feel marriage is the proper response, the honorable thing to do. This is in face of the fact that the highest divorce rate group is teenagers who marry when she's pregnant. In spite of the collapse of their personal fable (she *is* pregnant), they maintain another personal fable about being married happily ever after. When confronted with the overwhelming statistics of divorce and/or abuse in teenage pregnant marriages, a typical response is, "That won't happen to us, we're not a statistic."

A minister we know says he refuses to marry any pregnant teenage couple who comes to him until after the birth of the baby. Interestingly enough, he says, more than half of the couples never end up marrying. It seems a lot of such couples feel tremendous pressure, from parents predominantly, to get married. But once the baby comes, they realize that the world does not come to an end if there is no wedding.

So, if you're young, pregnant, and got engaged as a result, ask yourself: *Why am I marrying*? Is the answer based squarely on love, or on doing the honorable thing? Remember, two wrongs don't make a right.

Note: This page is reproduced from the Couple's Book.

ISSUES OF SPECIAL FOCUS

If these issues pertain to you, discuss them with your partner.

1. If I was abused as a child, or if my partner was, am I afraid that we may repeat the past and abuse our children? Why?

2. How do I get along with my/your children? How do you get along with my/your children? What would I change about this answer?

3. If we're already expecting a child, have we discussed the possibility of waiting until after the birth of the baby before we even consider marriage?

RELATIONSHIP CHECK

Each of you should circle the number that best represents how you are feeling about your relationship after discussing this topic. Remember, you each need to select your own number.

1. very close   2. somewhat close   3. somewhat distant   4. very distant

What would I want to discuss further with you about this topic?

_____
_____
_____
_____
_____
_____

PRE-MARITAL COUNSELING

In many Catholic dioceses, and some Protestant churches, there are policies regarding pre-marital counseling or evaluation. Typically such policies stipulate that a couple must receive counseling and/or an evaluation prior to the wedding if certain conditions are present.

These conditions may include pregnancy, youth (the couple is under 18 years of age), immaturity, or any other pastoral concern that the priest or minister may have about the couple's readiness for marriage. The purpose of pre-marital counseling is to help couples with special circumstances or problems to see more clearly some difficulties that may lie ahead, and to equip them better to make a mature Christian decision regarding their relationship. Like marriage preparation itself, pre-marital counseling is an opportunity for growth and enrichment.

Note: **This page is reproduced from the Couple's Book.**

Our Finances, Friends, Work, and Leisure Time

"Finances, friends, and fun—yes, I'd like all three, please." Unfortunately, all three can grow into problems for a married couple if they don't communicate about them. This chapter ties in the three areas, touching also on jobs and careers, and challenges the couple to be specific in their expectations.

The budget worksheet is a favorite exercise among engaged couples. Before they get into it though, stress that the process of budget planning is just as important as the end result. In other words, how they communicate and treat each other during the budget planning is just as important as the budget itself.

It is suggested that team members go to banks and insurance agents and obtain brochures and other forms of information on renter's insurance, homeowners insurance, auto and life insurance, various savings and checking accounts, I.R.A.s, C.D.s, and other annuities and funds. Place these on a table so the couples can take what they want during a break in the program.

In speaking on finances, shy away from the nuts and bolts of finances, and stick more to the interpersonal, relational aspects on how to communicate on finances. In your group of engaged couples you may have a 35-year-old C.P.A. sitting next to an 18-year-old secretarial student who doesn't know how to write a check. You can't meet all the needs of such a wide range of experience. And yet they all have one common need: to hear a married couple talk about how they handle finances in their relationship. Success is not determined by the amount of money made, but by how the marriage is strengthened and communication increased.

Friends and the use of leisure time is sometimes a sore issue for couples. Anyone who's worked with engaged couples has heard one partner complain about the other's friends, or the boys-night out, or the lack of fun time they spend with each other. We may be tempted to discount or minimalize such complaints from the engaged. Don't! If they're having a hard time now with their separate friends and the use of, or lack of, leisure time, then how will it change once they are married? It may get worse. They need to discuss all this thoroughly, to the satisfaction of each. You can help by encouraging them to stay focused on it and not to trivialize the topic themselves through jokes or silence.

Our Finances, Friends, Work, and Leisure Time
Talk Outline

1. Introduce self and topic
- Number of years married?
- Any children? Ages?
- Town you live in? Church?
- How long involved as a marriage preparation volunteer couple?
- Any other general information about yourselves?
- What's your topic?
- Why is it important for them, as engaged couples, to hear about this topic?

2. The A–B–C–D of handling finances (without ruining your marriage)
- A=Appreciation! of what you have materially, of what income you have, and of each other. It's fine to have future goals and to improve your standard of living. However, don't forget to be thankful for what you have *now*—enjoy life now!
- B=Budget! List out sources of income vs debt/expenses. Refer to budget planner in engaged couple's workbook.
- C=Communication! Practice good communication skills when discussing finances. Listen to each other. Work as a team, not as opponents.
- D=Discipline! Both partners have to understand and be committed to working through financial matters. Both have to be willing to sacrifice, share and/or surrender ones "wants" in order to pay for our "needs." (*Note:* You may consider presenting these in reverse order, D–C–B–A.)

3. Insurance: health, major medical, life, dental, auto, home, or renters'. Discuss these at length. For example:
- Health—essential. Typically a benefit offered by an employer.
- Major medical—same as health.
- Life—not essential, but highly advisable especially if you have or are expecting children. Along this topic, consider having wills drawn up by an attorney. Some see this as morbid, others see it as "peace of mind." Usually young couples do not see a need for wills. Suggest that they are worth more than they think.
- Dental—nice benefit from employer if offered, but not necessary.
- Auto—Check the requirements of the state you live in. Discuss the necessary coverages.

4. Credit. Discuss the appeal of credit cards and "no payment until June" loans and the financial consequences

5. Charity and stewardship. Discuss the importance of giving to those who are in greater need than we are and of supporting our parish community

NOTES:
1. Read the couple's and leader's edition chapters on this topic.
2. Lace this and all talks with personal stories, examples, and anecdotes that add color and/or demonstrate what you are talking about.

Notes

Chapter 7
Our Finances, Friends, Work, and Leisure Time

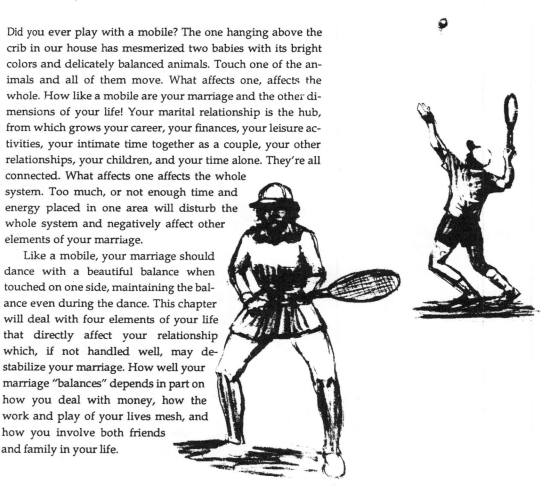

Did you ever play with a mobile? The one hanging above the crib in our house has mesmerized two babies with its bright colors and delicately balanced animals. Touch one of the animals and all of them move. What affects one, affects the whole. How like a mobile are your marriage and the other dimensions of your life! Your marital relationship is the hub, from which grows your career, your finances, your leisure activities, your intimate time together as a couple, your other relationships, your children, and your time alone. They're all connected. What affects one affects the whole system. Too much, or not enough time and energy placed in one area will disturb the whole system and negatively affect other elements of your marriage.

Like a mobile, your marriage should dance with a beautiful balance when touched on one side, maintaining the balance even during the dance. This chapter will deal with four elements of your life that directly affect your relationship which, if not handled well, may destabilize your marriage. How well your marriage "balances" depends in part on how you deal with money, how the work and play of your lives mesh, and how you involve both friends and family in your life.

Note: **This page is reproduced from the Couple's Book.**

For many couples finances are an area of conflict. Although making a lot of money may make life easier, not making a lot of money is rarely the actual cause for conflict. Rather, conflict arises over how couples manage their money. Different expectations, assumptions, and priorities lead to different styles of fiscal management. We recommend two basic things: First, *have a budget*. Agree on it and stick to it! Second, *communicate* with each other about your budget, your finances, your worries, and your hopes.

It never ceases to amaze us how couples fail to communicate on this topic. We've known couples who don't even know what each partner makes in salary! Others divide their money between "his" and "hers" with no allotment for "ours." One such couple took turns purchasing the common major items they needed, which resulted in a house furnished with "her" couch, "his" TV, "her" end tables, "his" coffee table, "her" kitchen table, and so on. Their reasoning: if they divorce, it'll be easy to figure out who gets what!

Typically, couples with few problems based on money are those who have a healthy, on-going line of communication. They have joint accounts and each partner knows what's coming in and going out. Each may take a different role such as bill payer, salary check depositor, banker, and/or checkbook balancer, but they keep each other informed. One does not make major purchases without the agreement of the other.

Good communication helps couples "balance" work and play as well. Until recently, the prevailing work ethic emphasized work over leisure. Being with your family and having fun were granted the time that was "left over" from one's true purpose in life: *to work!*

A recent trend in career counseling reflects more current attempts to view our lives as a whole, made up of many parts. Career counselors advise job seekers to consider all aspects of their lives, work play, family, and friends when choosing or changing a career. The premise is that your career (loosely defined as the type of work you pursue) should be a part of your overall lifestyle. Thirty years ago, marriages and families had to conform to the husband's job. Today, couples are rightfully seeking careers that harmoniously con-

---

MR. MOM

Today in the United States more men are assuming the role of homemaker, primary childcare provider, or "domestic engineer." According to the Bureau of Labor Statistics, over 257,000 husbands stay home to care for the kids while the wives work outside the home. Economic opportunity for the family, career opportunity for the wife and the desire of fathers to care for their children full time are typically the guiding force behind the growth in the number of "Mr. Moms."

The U.S. census bureau reports that the fastest growing segment of the workforce today is married mothers of young children. The wife may be able to earn significantly more than the husband, and thus will find herself kissing both hubbie and baby good-bye in the morning as she heads for the office.

Men are finding that they can be the primary care-giving parent and not relinquish any sense of masculinity or self-worth. And, in fact, those daddies who do stay home with young children typically find it a nurturing and enriching experience.

Regardless of who assumes the role of primary childcare provider, studies show that there is a trend in the U.S. for both parents to be actively involved in the raising of children. And children whose fathers and mothers are equally involved in all aspects tend to grow up more self-confident and emotionally and psychologically well adjusted.

66

Note: This page is reproduced from the Couple's Book.

nect with their private family lives.

These ideas are reflected in our attempts to achieve a "balance" of work and play in our lives. Some people have no problem playing and may need to concentrate more on work. Others, regulated by the "work ethic," need to learn the value of play and spontaneity! Marriages, new and old, need humor, playfulness, laughter, dancing, joking. Choosing a particular career or re-evaluating the one you already have can create more time to spend with your partner, adding new and life-giving experiences to your relationship.

Your relationship with your friends will probably change once you are married, especially if they are not married. While old friends aren't dropped just because you marry, some become "our" friends once they get to know you as a couple, and others may naturally fade away. You may also find that some do remain "his" or "her" friends and are, along with the other kinds of friendships, life giving and not destructive to your relationship. An occasional "boys night out" or "girls night out" is fine, but not on a regular basis. This may be a difficult adjustment at first, but it's a necessary change for the long term health of your marriage.

Many couples marry because they get along, find each other attractive and interesting, and "can live with each other." But when they need to talk about something important, they turn to a friend for support. Eventually these couples find they are out of touch and have grown apart. We believe that husbands and wives need to be best friends, able to communicate about all facets of their lives so that, like the mobile, the individual gifts each brings to the marriage achieve the rhythm and grace of elements that work well together.

WOMEN (AND MEN) IN THE WORKPLACE

A 1991 government research team report, "Women at Thirtysomething," concluded that American women are underpaid and unappreciated, even though they've obtained a higher level of education and training than women in western Europe and Japan. The report also found that unemployment in the U.S. is higher for women than for men, no matter what degree they have. And finally, in only seven of 33 major occupations did women receive pay equal to their male counterparts.

Traditionally men were the "breadwinners" and women the "homemakers." And if a woman sought employment, it was conceived as a supplement to the man's income. Currently, however, women are seeking long-term careers beyond traditional jobs. Instead of becoming nurses or grade school teachers, women are finding less traditional work in telecommunications, engineering, finances, and politics.

Unfortunately, our society resists women's changing role in the world of work. In general, women often feel a lack of support from family and friends, both men and women, for their career pursuits. This will change with time. But as a couple about to marry, it is important that you discuss in detail the woman's as well as the man's career, and what effect both might have on your marriage and family life.

Note: This page is reproduced from the Couple's Book.

His Page

Answer these questions by yourself and then share your answers with your partner.

1. In what ways is money a source of conflict for us? What would I like to change?_____
_____
_____

2. Who managed the money in my family of origin?_____
_____
_____

3. What, if any, concerns do I have about how you spend money?_____
_____
_____

4. My chief goal for five years from now _____
_____
_____

5. My "ideal" house is _____
_____
_____

6. What, if any, concerns do I have about any of your friends or mine?_____
_____
_____

7. Am I content with how we spend our free time? What would I change?_____
_____
_____

8. My "ideal" vacation is _____
_____
_____

9. Am I content with how our jobs/careers affect our relationship? Why?_____
_____
_____

69

Note: **This page is reproduced from the Couple's Book.**

His Financial Worksheet

Complete this worksheet by yourself. Discuss your answers with your partner,
and then together complete "Our Financial Worksheet."

1. What is our present combined monthly net income? $_____.

2. What are our combined present assets? $_____

_____ checking account(s)	_____ real estate (house, condo, townhouse, etc.)
_____ saving account(s)	_____ clothing
_____ C.D.s/stocks/savings	_____ jewelry
_____ cars/trucks/vans	_____ others:_____;_____;_____;_____.
_____ furniture / appliance	

Total: $_____

3. How much do I think we should spend a month on the following items?

HOUSING: $_____   TRANSPORTATION: $_____

_____ mortgage/rent	_____ car payments
_____ insurance & tax	_____ insurance & taxes
_____ utilities & fuel	_____ gas & maintenance
_____ phone	_____ repairs
_____ maintenance/repairs	_____ public transportation
_____ home decorating & miscellaneous	

FOOD: $_____   CLOTHING & PERSONAL CARE: $_____

_____ groceries	_____ his
_____ liquor, beer	_____ hers
_____ tobacco	_____ kids
	_____ cosmetics,haircuts,etc.

FUN & LEISURE: $_____   INSURANCE: $_____

_____ eating out	_____ medical/hospitalization
_____ movies/videos	_____ life insurance
_____ hobbies	_____ retirement
_____ sports events	

CHARGES, LOANS, INSTALLMENTS, MISCELLANEOUS: $_____

_____ furniture	_____ credit cards	_____ educational loans/expenses
_____ wedding rings	_____ pets	_____ donations & charity
_____ alimony/child care	_____ savings	_____ memberships / subscriptions
		_____ other:_____

4. TOTAL MONTHLY EXPENSES: _____   vs TOTAL MONTHLY INCOME: _____

_____
70

Note: This page is reproduced from the Couple's Book.

Her Page

Answer these questions by yourself and then share your answers with your partner.

1. In what ways is money a source of conflict for us? What would I like to change?_____
_____
_____

2. Who managed the money in my family of origin?_____
_____
_____

3. What, if any, concerns do I have about how you spend money?_____
_____
_____

4. My chief goal for five years from now is...._____
_____
_____

5. My "ideal" house is _____
_____
_____

6. What, if any, concerns do I have about any of your friends or mine?_____
_____
_____

7. Am I content with how we spend our free time? What would I change?_____
_____
_____

8. My "ideal" vacation is _____
_____
_____

9. Am I content with how our jobs/careers affect our relationship? Why?_____
_____
_____

71

Note: This page is reproduced from the Couple's Book.

Her Financial Worksheet

Complete this worksheet by yourself. Discuss your answers with your partner,
and then together complete "Our Financial Worksheet."

1. What is our present combined monthly net income? $_____.
2. What are our combined present assets? $_____   _____ real estate (house, condo, townhouse, etc.)

_____ checking account(s)   _____ clothing

_____ saving account(s)   _____ jewelry

_____ C.D.s/stocks/savings   _____ others:_____;_____;_____;_____.

_____ cars/trucks/vans

_____ furniture / appliance

Total: $_____

3. How much do I think we should spend a month on the following items?

HOUSING: $_____   TRANSPORTATION: $_____

_____ mortgage/rent   _____ car payments

_____ insurance & tax   _____ insurance & taxes

_____ utilities & fuel   _____ gas & maintenance

_____ phone   _____ repairs

_____ maintenance/repairs   _____ public transportation

_____ home decorating & miscellaneous

FOOD: $_____   CLOTHING & PERSONAL CARE: $_____

_____ groceries   _____ his

_____ liquor, beer   _____ hers

_____ tobacco   _____ kids

                                     _____ cosmetics,haircuts,etc.

FUN & LEISURE: $_____   INSURANCE: $_____

_____ eating out   _____ medical/hospitalization

_____ movies/videos   _____ life insurance

_____ hobbies   _____ retirement

_____ sports events

CHARGES, LOANS, INSTALLMENTS, MISCELLANEOUS: $_____

_____ furniture   _____ credit cards   _____ educational loans/expenses

_____ wedding rings   _____ pets   _____ donations & charity

_____ alimony/child care _____ savings   _____ memberships / subscriptions

                                                       _____ other:_____

4.   TOTAL MONTHLY EXPENSES: _____   vs TOTAL MONTHLY INCOME:_____

Note: **This page is reproduced from the Couple's Book.**

Our Financial Worksheet

After you have discussed your individual answers on the His and Her worksheets, complete this worksheet as a couple. If you run into disagreements, don't worry. It may take awhile before you can come to an agreement on some issues. Just remember to use good communication and fair fighting skills in your discussions!

*What is our present combined monthly net income?_____

*What do we think we should spend monthly on the following items?

HOUSING: $_____   TRANSPORTATION: $_____

_____mortgage/rent   _____car payments

_____insurance & tax   _____insurance & taxes

_____utilities & fuel   _____gas & maintenance

_____phone   _____repairs

_____maintenance/repairs   _____public transportation

_____home decorating & miscellaneous

FOOD: $_____   CLOTHING & PERSONAL CARE: $_____

_____groceries   _____his

_____liquor, beer   _____hers

                                _____kids'

                                _____cosmetics,haircuts,etc

FUN & LEISURE: $_____   INSURANCE: $_____

_____eating out   _____medical/hospitalization

_____movies/videos   _____life insurance

_____hobbies   _____retirement

_____sports events

CHARGES, LOANS, INSTALLMENTS, MISCELLANEOUS: $_____

_____furniture   _____credit cards   _____educational loans/expenses

_____wedding rings   _____pets   _____donations & charity

_____alimony/child care _____savings   _____memberships / subscriptions

                                              _____other:_____

4. TOTAL MONTHLY EXPENSES: _____   vs TOTAL MONTHLY INCOME:_____

1. Where were the areas of disagreement?
2. Where did you each need to compromise?
3. How do you feel about your financial situation?

73

Note: This page is reproduced from the Couple's Book.

GROUP SECTION

Discuss this case study with other couples in a small group.

Mark and Linda each hold a job, making a total of $40,000 a year. They live in a nice home with a combined monthly mortgage, taxes, and house insurance payments that eat up 33% of their take-home pay. They charge purchases like household items, clothes, and electronic equipment and entertainment expenses, spending their cash on food and extras. They have 8 credit cards. Savings and investments are a low priority for them.

1. What concerns do you have for Mark and Linda's financial situation?
2. What could be the potential dangers?
3. What changes would you suggest to them?

ISSUES OF SPECIAL FOCUS

If these issues pertain to you, discuss them with your partner.

1. If one or both of us were married before, what difficult situations may, or already have arisen concerning old friends from the previous marriage(s)? How will we handle such difficulties?
2. If one or both of us have children already, have we discussed how our new blended family will deal with tighter financial constraints?
3. If we're presently expecting a baby, how will we juggle child care, our job(s), and financial demands?

RELATIONSHIP CHECK

Each of you should circle the number that best represents how you are feeling about your relationship after discussing this topic. Remember, you each need to select your own number.

       1. very close   2. somewhat close   3. somewhat distant   4. very distant

What might I want to discuss further with you about this topic? Discuss your individual answers.

_____
_____
_____
_____
_____
_____
_____

Note: This page is reproduced from the Couple's Book.

Chapter 8

Our Spirituality

Along with communication, spirituality is the most important topic for an engaged couple to discuss. It is not only an important topic, but a wide topic. It includes sacramentality, religion, faith, church, and personal beliefs—all of which are connected yet separate. It would take a separate workbook to cover all this in depth. In this chapter we try to cover all of it to various degrees. Less you, a team member, become overwhelmed (and thus discouraged) by the breath and depth of this topic, remember the following:

Just by the mere fact that you walk into the room as a married couple, obviously committed not only to your own marriage but also to the welfare of others, you have given the best lesson on couple spirituality to the engaged. Your participation as a married couple in the marriage preparation process provides a great witness for the engaged couples. As the authors of *Preparing For Marriage: A Study of Marriage Preparations in American Catholic Dioceses* (St. Meinrad, Ind.: Abbey Press, 1983) state: "...we found it reassuring that clergy and laity are working together in most marriage preparation programs. Couples are not only being prepared for marriage but are also being offered a model and an experience of church in the process."

This is why it is so important to have married couples run marriage preparation programs. The sign value is very great, indeed. Any couple's marriage is a journey of faith, a journey that begins with the preparation process. Ideally, a couple will grow spiritually during this brief process. According to *Faithful to Each Other Forever: A Catholic Handbook of Pastoral Help for Marriage Preparation* (1989 USCC), one of the goals of marriage preparation should be "the identification and deepening of the couple's faith." You help facilitate this by just being present at the program as a married couple.

In this chapter there is an emphasis on the personal beliefs and spiritualities of the individual person and couple. The goal of the session is to get the couple to reflect on this and discover that faith element. Most engaged couples are at that stage of faith development in which they are still wrestling with basic questions about their own beliefs. In general, they tend to reject, or at least be apathetic to, religion and its institutions. After several years of marriage, they will mature in their faith. But, generally speaking, at this stage it's enough to get them talking about some of the more primary elements of their spirituality.

Be careful not to evangelize, preach, or "talk down" to the engaged couples. As with the other topics in this book, the team couple is to speak about their own stories. Their presentation on spirituality can present some of the concepts of sacramentality, faith, and religious teachings, but the emphasis should be on the discovery of the couple to the presence of God in their lives.

Finally, the role of Jesus in a couple's married life needs to be addressed. It is obvious, and yet so often overlooked: if the couple is seeking a sacramental marriage in the church, this presupposes some degree of faith in Jesus. You are not to measure the faith readiness of any couple. How could you? Rather, you are to assume, and build on the faith present in each individual. Remember, the most cynical looking couple in your group may in fact be the most faith-filled.

Our Spirituality
Talk Outline

1. Introduce self and topic
- Number of years married?
- Any children? Ages?
- Town you live in? Church?
- How long involved as a marriage preparation volunteer couple?
- Any other general information about yourselves?
- What's your topic?
- Why is it important for them, as engaged couples, to hear about this topic?

2. Marital spirituality. A very broad topic covering a wide spectrum of issues; not just a "church thing."
We'll cover 2 major aspects of your spirituality as a couple: religion and relationship.

3. Spirituality, the relationship that you have with God
- It means recognizing God's presence in your life and developing a relationship with this God through prayer, church participation, or other means.
- It means living in accord with your understanding of God's plan for your life.
- It means becoming one and living out to the fullest, the Sacrament that you are.
- It also means accepting your role as steward or caretaker of the earth, animals, and humanity. Here it is your responsibility as a creation of God to feed the hungry, clothe the naked, and shelter the homeless.

4. Religion refers to
- your religious identity (Christian, Jewish, Muslim, etc.).
- the denomination you belong to (Roman Catholic, Lutheran, Episcopalian, Methodist, etc.).
- worship—how, when, where, why and with whom you do it.
- rituals—what, where when, why, how, and with whom you do them.
- beliefs—what you believe about God, Jesus, the church, etc.

5. Relationship
The quality of your relationships exhibits for yourself and for others the quality of your response to God's presence in your life and to your acceptance of your role as steward. These relationships include:
- your relationship with God.
- your relationship with each other.
- your relationship with a community that shares common experiences, values, worship, and faith.

6. Blending of religion and relationships in a marriage, and especially in an interfaith marriage, needs to be handled in the following ways:
- loving—accepting each other unconditionally
- respectfully—valuing each other's opinions, thoughts, and feelings
- with good communication skills—listening and asking appropriate questions
- with trust and openness
- with effort and sincerity in trying to find an agreed upon common ground that both partners can embrace and accept.

NOTES:

1. Read the couple's and leader's edition chapters on this topic.

2. Lace this and all talks with personal stories, examples, and anecdotes that add color and/or demonstrate what you are talking about.

Notes

Chapter 8
Our Spirituality

When Mike and Jean announced their engagement, her parents were relieved. Jean had been seriously dating another man who was Protestant. Her parents, devout Catholics, were uncomfortable with the idea of their daughter in a "mixed marriage." They had hoped and prayed that Jean would marry someone like Mike, someone with the same faith. And now their wish had come true.

Unfortunately, Jean's parents actually were not getting what they wanted. Their daughter is indeed marrying an-

Note: This page is reproduced from the Couple's Book.

other Catholic. But that is no guarantee that Jean and Mike have a similar "faith." Their marriage, like most marriages, will be a "mixed" marriage. Each of them has had a different experience of religion, a different spirituality, and a different perspective of the role of Christ, and God, in their lives. So while both indeed call themselves Catholic, they may mean very different things.

To one degree or another, we are all "interfaith" couples, regardless of whether or not we have been raised in or practice the same faith. We can testify to this in our own marriage. We were each born and raised Roman Catholic, and therefore we share many similar experiences and memories. However, our individual relationships with God are quite different. Each of our approaches to prayer, to Jesus, to church, to the holiness of our surroundings, are marked by subtle and some not so subtle differences. Over the years we have discovered that while we each can continue our individual spiritualities, we are also able to combine the two to form "our" spirituality as a couple. Such diversity within a similar religious tradition is a wonderful thing! It has added tremendously to the vitality of our marriage and to the depths of our individual experiences of God.

Discovering your spirituality as a couple takes time. But like all aspects of your relationship, it will develop and grow. Communicating about your own spirituality honestly and lovingly opens the way to a relationship with God that best reflects who the two of you are as a couple.

The foundation of your marital spirituality is the individual experiences, beliefs, and perceptions that you each bring to your relationship. A good way to start to uncover and identify these is to answer the following question: "In the midst of great joy or sorrow, where do I find God?" That is a thought-provoking question to answer. We suggest you wrestle with it and discuss it with your partner. This will help your partner understand more about your unique relationship with God and will ultimately lead to your new spirituality as a couple.

As with most of the issues affecting your relationship, your relationship with God has been influenced by your fam-

INTERFAITH MARRIAGES

Marriages within the church in which a Catholic marries a non-Catholic are commonplace today. A 1981 study by the United States Catholic Conference, "Empirical Research on Interfaith Marriages in America," concluded that:

1. Attitudes toward interfaith marriages are becoming more favorable;

2. The rate of interfaith marriages will continue to grow;

3. For every interfaith marriage that remains mixed, there is one in which one spouse converts to the other's religion;

4. Nearly all conversions take place at the time of marriage or before the first child is ten years old;

5. Continued religious differences within a marriage tend to reduce marital satisfaction and decrease church involvement;

6. The mother usually has a stronger influence on the children's religious identification than the father;

7. Disagreement over children's religious upbringing is one of the most common causes of strife in interfaith marriages;

8. Interfaith marriages have a higher percentage of divorce than same-faith marriages.

One point not mentioned on this list is the potential that interfaith marriages have to enrich their church and community. An interfaith couple who possess a loving, nonjudgmental relationship can be a symbol of acceptance and cooperation for all to see.

76

Note: This page is reproduced from the Couple's Book.

ily. As we explained in Chapter Four, you are a product of your upbringing. Therefore, your spirituality is a product of the spirituality of your family of origin. This doesn't mean that what you do and what your parents do are identical, but that there are similarities. The family has been called the "domestic church," for out of our family life springs the worshiping practices and faith of every individual. It is within our families that we first experienced love and tenderness, and that we first learned to pray. And it was within our family's life that we first experienced the love of God through our love for each other. Family life is sacred. When most of us reflect back on our family lives, it's hard to believe that anything so ordinary as the daily routine of getting food on the table and raising children could possibly be holy. Yet we believe it is. Jesus' birth into a family was not mere coincidence. It is within the family that the sacred in the ordinary is found, and we rediscover the love of God which unites us all.

Choosing to be married in the Catholic church means that you are accepting the responsibilities of living out a sacramental marriage. And what does that mean? Living a sacramental marriage means that you and your partner make a covenant with God to live a life that reflects to the world the love of God. The Bible compares the love of a wife and a husband to the love that God has for God's people. Your responsibility then is to love each other unconditionally, as God loves us.

Most people believe that the priest marries you. This is not true. The real ministers of your sacrament are the two of you. During the wedding ceremony, when you give your mutual consent, you marry each other. In this way marriage is the unique sacrament among the seven. And it further emphasizes the point that being married in the church is something not to be taken lightly. Ask yourself again why you are about to have a church wedding. Is it because of parental pressure? Or because it will look good? Or because you always dreamed of being married in a church? Or is it because you value your faith and want to live out that faith in a covenant relationship with your partner and God within

---

DIVORCE AND ANNULMENT

The commonly held belief that the Roman Catholic church does not allow divorce at all is incorrect. Divorce is allowed, but in such a few restricted situations, it is safe to state that, generally, divorce is not allowed in the church.

Many confuse divorce and annulment. Some believe that annulments are simply church divorces. But according to church teaching, there is a very real difference between divorce and annulment. An annulment is an official church declaration that a valid sacramental marriage never existed in the first place. A divorce is a civil declaration that a valid marriage did exist, but has now ended.

There are many grounds for a church annulment. Some are: lack of maturity at the time of the wedding; lack of proper form, i.e. the presence of a priest or deacon and two witnesses; moral impotency; failure of being open to having children; prior intention to be unfaithful; psychopathology and/or schizophrenia; psychic incompetence; prior alcoholism or addiction.

However, the number one ground for annulments is the lack of discretion; in other words, the individual(s) did not understand the nature of living out a sacramental marriage at the time of the wedding.

Annulments are handled through the Tribunal of each diocese. The annulment process can take from a few months to a few years and may cost several hundred dollars to complete. Two myths which need to be dispelled are: (1) Children from an annulled marriage are *not* considered illegitimate, and (2) civilly divorced Catholics who remarry without an annulment are *not* automatically excommunicated. For more information, contact the Tribunal in your diocese.

77

Note: This page is reproduced from the Couple's Book.

the context of a worshipping community? By seeking a church wedding you are making a decision to live out a sacramental marriage, which means you are committing yourself to a permanent, exclusive relationship of love and responsibility with your partner.

ROMANCING EARTH

"Recycle, Reuse, Reduce." These are the three "R's" of our environmentally conscious society today. As a culture, we are suddenly becoming more aware of our responsibility to Mother Earth, and are making collective and individual attempts to become better stewards of our precious planet.

A steward is someone who is responsible for the safety and well-being of that which has been given. A steward oversees that the use of this "given" is prudent, caring, life-giving. A steward realizes that you don't truly own, but rather are just temporarily responsible. God has assigned us to be stewards of our planet.

Our stewardship should dictate that we drop our consumer mentality and adopt a relationship mentality with the land, water, air, and animals. As with your relationship as a young couple in love, our relationship with the environment should be characterized by a healthy give and take, respect and selfless love. The hallmark of a young couple's relationship is romance. Your partner is precious to you; you treat your partner with tenderness. We would do well to model our relationship with Mother Earth on our relationship with one we love, and maintain the romance with Mother Earth.

Note: This page is reproduced from the Couple's Book.

His Page

Answer these questions by yourself. When you are finished share them with your partner.

1. When I was a child, my family of origin: (check all that apply)

☐ went to Mass/Worship Service every Sunday

☐ went 1 or 2 times a month

☐ went a couple of times a year

☐ placed a high priority on our faith

☐ read the Bible

☐ prayed together

☐ had little to do with religion, church, or faith

2. How important is my faith to me (circle one):

      1. very important   2. somewhat important   3. not important

3. Why am I getting married in the church?

_____

_____

_____

4. Do I know what you think about God? Jesus?

_____

_____

5. How important is it for me to raise our children in my faith?

_____

_____

6. Do I think that God has a place in our marriage? What is it?

_____

_____

_____

7. Is religion a source of conflict for us?

_____

_____

_____

79

Note: This page is reproduced from the Couple's Book.

8. When I think about our marriage as a sacrament, I feel

_____

_____

9. I have felt that God has been present in my life, usually when

_____

_____

_____

10. In the midst of great joy or sorrow, where do I find God?

_____

_____

_____

_____

11. If Jesus had one day to spend with us what would we do?

_____

_____

_____

_____

What would we talk about?

_____

_____

_____

_____

What would he say to us about our love and our relationship?

_____

_____

_____

_____

What would he want to teach us?

_____

_____

_____

_____

Note: This page is reproduced from the Couple's Book.

Her Page

Answer these questions by yourself. When you are finished share them with your partner.

1. When I was a child, my family of origin: (check all that apply)

☐   went to Mass/Worship Service every Sunday

☐   went 1 or 2 times a month

☐   went a couple of times a year

☐   placed a high priority on our faith

☐   read the Bible

☐   prayed together

☐   had little to do with religion, church, or faith

2. How important is my faith to me (circle one):

        1. very important   2. somewhat important   3. not important

3. Why am I getting married in the church?

_____
_____
_____

4. Do I know what you think about God? Jesus?

_____
_____

5. How important is it for me to raise our children in my faith?

_____
_____

6. Do I think that God has a place in our marriage? What is it?

_____
_____
_____

7. Is religion a source of conflict for us?

_____
_____
_____

Note: This page is reproduced from the Couple's Book.

8. When I think about our marriage as a sacrament, I feel

_____

_____

9. I have felt that God has been present in my life, usually when

_____

_____

_____

10. In the midst of great joy or sorrow, where do I find God?

_____

_____

_____

_____

11. If Jesus had one day to spend with us what would we do?

_____

_____

_____

_____

What would we talk about?

_____

_____

_____

_____

What would he say to us about our love and our relationship?

_____

_____

_____

_____

What would he want to teach us?

_____

_____

_____

_____

82

Note: This page is reproduced from the Couple's Book.

GROUP SECTION

1. If Jesus were to return today as a married individual, what kind of relationship would he have with his wife? How would Jesus settle a disagreement with his wife?

2. What is the difference between organized religion and faith?

3. Discuss whether religious traditions and rituals should be an important part of your future marriage and family life.

ISSUES OF SPECIAL FOCUS

If you are a Catholic and non-Catholic couple, discuss these questions:

1. How does the partner who is non-Catholic feel about having a Catholic church wedding?

2. How do each of you feel about the Catholic partner having to promise to raise the children in the Catholic faith? Will you do it?

3. How will you celebrate the holidays if the non-Catholic partner is not Christian? For example, will you have a Christmas tree?

RELATIONSHIP CHECK

1. Each of you should circle the number that best represents how you feel about your relationship after discussing this topic. Remember, you each need to select your own number.

      1. very close   2. somewhat close   3. somewhat distant   4. very distant

2. What would I want to discuss further with you about this topic?

_____
_____
_____
_____
_____
_____
_____
_____
_____

Note: This page is reproduced from the Couple's Book.

Planning Our Wedding Liturgy

Let's look at two imaginary couples, each with an opposing, extreme attitude toward their wedding liturgies. Couple A could not care less about their wedding ceremony. They are really more into preparing for the wedding reception: which hors d'oeuvres to have, who to invite, what band to hire, how to deal with Uncle Henry when he has had too much to drink, and so on. They plan to leave the wedding preparation "stuff" to the priest—the selection of the readings, the responses, the hymns, and even the wording of the wedding vows— since he's the "pro" anyway.

Couple Z, the other extreme, wants the perfect wedding liturgy in which everything has a private meaning to them. The songs will be "their songs." The readings will be from their favorite poems. They want everything to symbolize their unique love for each other, and they want to softly whisper their vows to each other since it is the ultimate symbolic expression of their love.

Couple A is apathetic regarding their wedding liturgy and would be happy with a generic, "canned" Mass. Couple Z wants such a personal experience that they really don't need anyone else to be present. Now neither of these extreme couples represent you, of course—but do they?

Between these two extreme cases is a continuum of acceptable ways to approach your wedding liturgy. Here are a few ideas for you to consider.

Nuptial Mass?

The first and probably most significant decision you should make is whether you wish to have your wedding ceremony within the Liturgy of the Eucharist or outside of it, with Mass or without Mass. The wedding without a Mass may be the best ceremony for you if, for example, one of you is not Catholic. Both ceremonies would be the same up to and including the Rite of Matrimony. But they differ after that, as you can see from the following outlines.

Personal or Private Ceremony?

It is your wedding liturgy. Get involved! Be active in selecting the music, the responses, the readings and prayers that will be part of the ceremony. But also remember that it is a liturgy, which is public worship. So, although your wedding should be personal and have your distinctive touch, that does not mean that it should also be private; they are not the same thing. Your wedding should be personal and public; it should have your personal mark, but it is also the public proclamation of your love and lifelong commitment. The songs, prayers, and readings should have universal meaning so that all present are drawn into the service as participants and not just as observers.

Procession

More and more couples today no longer follow the custom of the father escorting the bride down the aisle to "give her away" to the groom, who has quietly entered the altar area by the side door. This custom has its roots in the days when young women were considered to be the property of the father, and thus were handed over to a new "owner," the groom. Even the veil over the bride's face can be traced to the days when marriages were contracted

Note: This page is reproduced from the Couple's Book.

Wedding Within Mass	Wedding Outside Mass

1. Introductory Rite
   a. Procession
   b. Opening prayer
	1. Introductory Rite
	   a. Procession
	   b. Opening prayer

2. Liturgy of the Word
   a. Hebrew Scripture (Old Testament) reading
   b. Psalm response
   c. Christian Scripture (New Testament) reading
   d. Gospel verse
   e. Gospel reading
   f. Homily, or sermon
	2. Liturgy of the Word
	   a. Hebrew Scripture (Old Testament) reading
	   b. Psalm response
	   c. Christian Scripture (New Testament) reading
	   d. Gospel verse
	   e. Gospel reading
	   f. Homily, or sermon

3. Rite of Marriage
   a. Exchange of vows
   b. Blessing of the rings and exchange of rings
   c. Couple's prayer
   d. Prayer of the Faithful
	3. Rite of Marriage
	   a. Exchange of vows
	   b. Blessing of the rings and exchange of rings
	   c. Couple's prayer
	   d. Prayer of the Faithful

4. Liturgy of Eucharist
   a. Preparation of the gifts
   b. Eucharistic Prayer
   c. Nuptial blessing
   d. Communion
	4. Nuptial Blessing
	
	5. Final Blessing

5. Concluding Rite and Final Blessing	

between families, and the groom did not even know what the bride looked like until the wedding day when the veil was lifted. You may want to consider some of the following alternatives for your wedding procession.

Have the bride's attendants and groom's attendants walk down the aisle together, followed by the groom and his parent(s), followed by the bride and her parent(s). Then both sets of parents present their children to each other. A second suggestion that is especially appropriate for couples who are older or who have been living out of their parents' home for some years is for the bride and groom to walk down the aisle together, without their parents accompanying them. Whatever you decide, just be certain that what you do is representative of you and your relationship, rather than because its the "expected" way of doing it.

Readings and Readers

There are typically two Bible readings. The First Reading is usually from the Hebrew Scriptures (Old Testament) and the Second Reading from the Christian Scriptures (New Testament). Later in this section we list all the Scripture readings from which you may select those you wish to be read during your wedding ceremony.

When selecting the Scripture passages, be sure to note what translation of the Bible will be used. All Scripture in this book is from the *Jerusalem Bible.* Discuss this with the priest or other appropriate person to make certain that the translation you prefer is used.

If the readers are to be friends or family members, stress that they are to practice by reading out loud in front of you as well as from a microphone if one is to be used at the church. Choose readers who will read well, project loud enough to be

Note: This page is reproduced from the Couple's Book.

heard, not be paralyzed by nervousness, and who will take this honor seriously.

Prayers
There are several options from which to choose. And as with most of your wedding liturgy preparations, we recommend that this be done with the help of the priest or liturgist. All your options are listed in this section. We recommend that the Lord's Prayer (Our Father), the universal prayer of all Christians, be recited and not sung, because each denomination has its own way of singing this prayer. To prevent confusion it would be easier for the community to recite it rather than sing it.

Wedding Vows
One of the ways that you can make your wedding unique is through the creation of your own vows. While there are commonly used forms, you have the option of writing your own. We suggest that you discuss this with the liturgist or priest to make sure that what you choose to say is compatible with the context of your wedding liturgy. You might also choose to memorize them and say them to each other without the assistance of the priest.

Music
Selecting appropriate music can be a difficult task for non-musicians. The parish music director, liturgist, organist, or the priest will be able to assist you in selecting music that will draw people into the ceremony, as well as be inspirational and meaningful to you and the church community. Since this is a religious ceremony, the music should be suitable for the worship of God. You may have a beautiful song in mind that would be better played at the reception than at the liturgy. There are hundreds of appropriate liturgical hymns and instrumentals from which to choose. If, however, you find that there are some songs that are so meaningful to you that you want them included in the liturgy, consider using them as people are entering the church and being seated. Also, you should consider what types of musical instruments you will need, such as an organ, a piano, a guitar or two, a flute or a harp. In addition, a leader of song or a cantor adds very much to the overall flow of the ceremony.

Liturgy Booklet
In a wedding liturgy booklet, you would list the order of the ceremony, including the words to all the prayers, responses, and songs that the congregation is to recite or sing. Such a booklet, distributed by the ushers, would be a guide to the ceremony and encourage the people to participate in it. In the booklet you may also list the names of the readers, priest(s)/minister(s), musicians, leader of song, attendants, and any personal message you may want to express to all your family and friends. You may also want to include your married names and new address. Remember to include in the booklet any special permission for the use of songs. Some publishers want specific information about their songs listed. The liturgist or music director would be able to assist you with this.

Photos and Videos
We suggest that you confer with the parish guidelines regarding the taking of photographs and videotaping. Your wedding is primarily a religious ceremony, an act of worship. Professional photographers and videotapers are welcome in most churches, but they have a restricted role and place. They should clearly understand where and when they are allowed to take pictures so that they do not detract from the central focus of the liturgy. Also consider whether you will be distracted by these people and their equipment. Will it make you uncomfortable, nervous, or act unnaturally? If so, consider modifying the number of people doing the shooting and focus more on what is central to this ceremony.

Final Thoughts
When selecting the readings and prayers for your wedding liturgy, remember to use inclusive language. For example, replace "mankind" with "humanity"or "all people." Instead of "What God has joined, let no man divide," you should substitute "What God has joined, let no one divide." Such sensitivity to inclusive language will reflect the equality in your relationship. As you select your readings and prayers, be mindful that the words in them refer to both of you. Discuss this with the priest so that he is sensitive to this as well.

87

Note: This page is reproduced from the Couple's Book.

Wedding Liturgy Planning Sheets

Two planning sheets for your wedding liturgy are provided. The draft copy is your working copy on which you should write your ideas, sharing them with the priest and/or parish liturgist, in order to make your final decisions regarding music, readings, prayers, responses, participants' role, and various other options. The final copy of your wedding liturgy planning sheet is where you should write the final selections for your wedding that both of you have agreed upon. This is the copy you should submit to the priest.

The pages following these two planning sheets list all the prayers, readings, and responses from which you may make your selections. Read each carefully, and then record the number and letter of the selection in the appropriate space on the planning sheet.

Note: **This page is reproduced from the Couple's Book.**

Wedding Liturgy Planning Sheet
(draft copy)

for _____ and _____
            (bride)   (groom)

Wedding date and time_____   Church_____

Rehearsal date and time_____   Priest/minister_____

Maid/matron of honor_____   Best man _____

Bride's attendants_____   _____

_____   _____

_____   _____

Groom's attendants_____   _____

_____   _____

_____   _____

Will the wedding be: Within Mass_____?   Outside Mass____?

Do we plan to have the following?

Organist	☐ Yes	☐ No	_____
Leader of song	☐ Yes	☐ No	_____
Other musicians	☐ Yes	☐ No	_____ _____
Ring bearer	☐ Yes	☐ No	_____
Flower girl	☐ Yes	☐ No	_____
Altar servers	☐ Yes	☐ No	_____ _____
Liturgy booklet	☐ Yes	☐ No	
Unity candle	☐ Yes	☐ No	
Eucharistic ministers	☐ Yes	☐ No	_____
Welcoming music	☐ Yes	☐ No	_____ _____
Musician(s)/singer(s)	☐ Yes	☐ No	_____

Introductory Rite

Processional hymn/music ☐ Yes ☐ No _____

Musician(s)/singer(s) ☐ Yes ☐ No _____ _____

Opening prayer (circle) 1 2 3 4   (page 93)

89

Note: This page is reproduced from the Couple's Book.

Liturgy of the Word

First reading # _____ (pages 94-96) Reader _____

Responsorial psalm # _____ (pages 97-99) Reader/singer _____

Second reading # _____ (pages 100-103) Reader _____

Gospel acclamation # _____ (page 103) Reader/singer _____

Gospel # _____ (pages 105-107)

Rite of Matrimony

Exchange of wedding vows: Consent (circle) 1 2 3 4 (pages 108-109)

Blessing of rings (circle) 1 2 3 (page 110)

Prayer of the couple yes___ no___ (page 111)

Prayer of the Faithful—indicate special intentions Reader_____

_____   _____

_____   _____

_____   _____

Liturgy of the Eucharist

Gift bearers _____   _____

Presentation hymn_____

Musician(s)/singer(s)_____ _____ _____

Prayer over the gifts (circle) 1 2 3 (page 113)

Preface (circle) 1 2 3 (page 114)

Nuptial blessing (circle) 1 2 3 (pages 115-116)

Communion hymn_____

Meditation hymn_____

Musician(s)/singer(s)_____

Prayer after communion (circle) 1 2 3 (page 117)

Concluding Rite

Final blessing (circle) 1 2 3 4 (pages 118-119)

Recessional hymn_____

Musician(s)/singer(s) _____ _____

_____ _____

Questions we need to ask, and things we need to do

_____   _____

_____   _____

_____   _____

90

Note: This page is reproduced from the Couple's Book.

Wedding Liturgy Planning Sheet
(final copy)

for _____ and _____
         (bride)   (groom)

Wedding date and time_____   Church_____
Rehearsal date and time_____   Priest/minister_____
Maid/matron of honor_____   Best man _____

Bride's attendants_____   _____
                  _____   _____
                  _____   _____

Groom's attendants_____   _____
                  _____   _____
                  _____   _____

Will the wedding be: Within Mass_____?   Outside Mass____?

Do we plan to have the following?

Organist	☐ Yes	☐ No	_____
Leader of song	☐ Yes	☐ No	_____
Other musicians	☐ Yes	☐ No	_____ _____
Ring bearer	☐ Yes	☐ No	_____
Flower girl	☐ Yes	☐ No	_____
Altar servers	☐ Yes	☐ No	_____ _____
Liturgy booklet	☐ Yes	☐ No	
Unity candle	☐ Yes	☐ No	
Eucharistic ministers	☐ Yes	☐ No	_____ _____
Welcoming music	☐ Yes	☐ No	_____ _____
Musician(s)/singer(s)	☐ Yes	☐ No	_____ _____

Introductory Rite
Processional hymn/music ☐ Yes   ☐ No _____
Musician(s)/singer(s) ☐ Yes   ☐ No _____   _____
Opening prayer (circle) 1 2 3 4   (page 93)

91

Note: This page is reproduced from the Couple's Book.

Liturgy of the Word

First reading # _____ (pages 94-96)   Reader _____

Responsorial psalm # _____ (pages 97-99)   Reader/singer _____

Second reading # _____ (pages 100-103)   Reader _____

Gospel acclamation (page104)   Reader/singer _____

Gospel # _____ (pages 105-107)

Rite of Matrimony

Exchange of wedding vows (circle) 1 2 3 4 (pages 108-109)

Blessing of rings (circle) 1 2 3 (page 109)

Prayer of the couple yes___ no___ (pages 109-110)

Prayer of the Faithful—indicate special intentions   Reader _____

_____   _____

_____   _____

_____   _____

Liturgy of the Eucharist

Gift bearers _____   _____

Presentation hymn_____

Musician(s)/singer(s)_____ _____ _____

Prayer over the gifts (circle) 1 2 3 (page 112)

Preface (circle) 1 2 3 (pages 112-113)

Nuptial blessing (circle) 1 2 3 (pages 113-115)

Communion hymn_____

Meditation hymn_____

Musician(s)/singer(s)_____

Prayer after communion (circle) 1 2 3 (page 115)

Concluding Rite

Final blessing (circle) 1 2 3 4 (pages 115-116)

Recessional hymn_____

Musician(s)/singer(s) _____ _____

_____ _____

Questions we need to ask, and things we need to do

_____   _____

_____   _____

_____   _____

____
92

Note: This page is reproduced from the Couple's Book.

Liturgy of the Word

Opening Prayer

Like any introduction or welcome, the opening prayer sets the tone for the rest of your wedding liturgy. You will find the selections available listed below. Read through each and select the one that you would like to have the priest and/or minister pray to begin your wedding liturgy. Choosing prayers and readings usually involves selecting a specific theme for the liturgy. As you read through these prayers, be sure to keep in mind the theme you have selected for your wedding. Themes such as love, covenant, faith, and hope are some of those commonly selected for weddings. Once you have decided on the theme, list your choices at the appropriate places on your planning sheet.

---

1. Father,
   you have made the bond of marriage
   a holy mystery,
   a symbol of Christ's love for his Church.
   Hear our prayers for N. and N.
   With faith in you and in each other
   they pledge their love today.
   May their lives always bear witness
   to the reality of that love.
   We ask you this
   through our Lord Jesus Christ, your Son,
   who lives and reigns with you and the Holy Spirit,
   one God, for ever and ever.

2. Father,
   hear our prayers for N. and N.
   who today are united in marriage before your altar.
   Give them your blessing,
   and strengthen their love for each other.
   We ask you this
   through our Lord…

3. Almighty God,
   hear our prayers for N. and N.,
   who have come here today
   to be united in the sacrament of marriage.
   Increase their faith in you and in each other,
   and through them bless your Church
   (with Christian children).
   We ask you this
   through our Lord…

4. Father,
   when you created mankind
   you willed that man and wife should be one.
   Bind N. and N.
   in the loving union of marriage;
   and make their love fruitful
   so that they may be living witnesses
   to your divine love in the world.
   We ask you this
   through our Lord…

93

Note: This page is reproduced from the Couple's Book.

First Reading

The first reading is typically taken from the Hebrew Scriptures (Old Testament). Throughout the Old Testament we read of God's great love for God's people, first in the book of Genesis, in the creation stories, and continuing on in stories of the love between a man and a woman.

Each of the selections here has its own message, its own theme. Read them carefully. Once you have made your selection, be certain that it fits the theme that you began in the opening prayer. Think too about who you would like to have read this. Would they read it well and convey its message? Once you have decided, list your choice at the appropriate place on your planning sheet.

---

1. A reading from the book of Genesis (1:26-28, 31a)

God said, "Let us make man in our own image, in the likeness of ourselves, and let them be masters of the fish of the sea, the birds of heaven, the cattle, all the wild beasts and all the reptiles that crawl upon the earth.

God created man in the image of himself,
in the image of God he created him,
male and female he created them.

God blessed them, saying to them, "Be fruitful, multiply, fill the earth and conquer it. Be masters of the fish of the sea, the birds of heaven and all living animals on the earth." God saw all he had made, and indeed it was very good.

2. A reading from the book of Genesis (2:18-24)

Yahweh God said, "It is not good that the man should be alone. I will make him a helpmate." So from the soil Yahweh God fashioned all the wild beasts and all the birds of heaven. These he brought to the man to see what he would call them; each one was to bear the name the man would give it. The man gave names to all the cattle, all the birds of heaven and all the wild beasts. But no helpmate suitable for man was found for him. So Yahweh God made the man fall into a deep sleep. And while he slept, he took one of his ribs and enclosed it in flesh. Yahweh God built the rib he had taken from the man into a woman, and brought her to the man. The man exclaimed:

"This at last is bone from my bones,

and flesh from my flesh!
This is to be called woman,
for this was taken from man."

This is why a man leaves his father and mother and joins himself to his wife, and they become one body.

3. A reading from the book of Genesis (24:48-51, 58-67)

The servant of Abraham said to Laban: "I blessed Yahweh God of my master Abraham, who had so graciously led me to choose the daughter of my master's brother for his son. Now tell me whether you are prepared to show kindness and goodness to my master; if not, say so, and I shall know what to do."

Laban and Bethuel replied, "This is from Yahweh; it is not in our power to say yes or no to you. Rebekah is there before you. Take her and go; and let her become the wife of your master's son, as Yahweh has decreed."

They called Rebekah and asked her, "Do you want to leave with this man?" "I do" she replied. Accordingly they let their sister Rebekah go, with her nurse, and Abraham's servant and his men. They blessed Rebekah in these words:

"Sisters of ours, increase
to thousands and tens of thousands!
May your descendants gain possession
of the gates of their enemies!"

Rebekah and her servants stood up, mounted the camels, and followed the man. The servant took Rebekah and departed. Isaac, who lived in the Ne-

Note: This page is reproduced from the Couple's Book.

geb, had meanwhile come into the wilderness of the well of Lahai Roi. Now Isaac went walking in the fields as evening fell, and looking up saw camels approaching. And Rebekah looked up and saw Isaac. She jumped down from her camel, and asked the servant, "Who is that man walking through the fields to meet us?" The servant replied, "That is my master"; then she took her veil and hid her face. The servant told Isaac the whole story, and Isaac led Rebekah into his tent and made her his wife; and he loved her. And so Isaac was consoled for the loss of his mother.

4. *A reading from the book of Tobit (7:9c-10, 11c-17)*

Then Tobias said to Raphael, "Brother Azarias, will you ask Raguel to give me my sister Sarah?" Raguel overheard the words, and said to the young man, "Eat and drink, and make the most of your evening; no one else has the right to take my daughter Sarah—no one but you, my brother. In any case, I, for my own part, am not at liberty to give her to anyone else, since you are her next of kin. However, my boy, I must be frank with you. "I have tried to find a husband for her seven times among our kinsmen, and all of them have died the first evening, on going to her room. But for the present, my boy, eat and drink; the Lord will grant you his grace and peace." Tobias spoke out, "I will not hear of eating and drinking till you have come to a decision about me." Raguel answered, "Very well. Since, as prescribed by the Book of Moses, she is given to you, heaven itself decrees she shall be yours. I therefore entrust your sister to you. From now you are her brother and she is your sister. She is given to you from today for ever. The Lord of heaven favor you tonight, my child, and grant you his grace and peace." Raguel called for his daughter Sarah, took her by the hand and gave her to Tobias with these words, "I entrust her to you; the law and the ruling recorded in the Book of Moses assign her to you as your wife. Take her; take her home to your father's house with a good conscience. The God of heaven grant you a good journey in peace." Then he turned to her mother and asked her to fetch him writing paper. He drew up the marriage contract, how he gave his daughter as bride to Tobias according to the ordinance in the Law of Moses. After this they began to eat and drink.

5. *A reading from the book of Tobit (8:4-9)*

Tobias rose from the bed, and said to Sarah, "Get up, my sister! You and I must pray and petition our Lord to win his grace and his protection. She stood up, and they began praying for protection, and this was how he began:

"You are blessed, O God of our fathers;
blessed, too, is your name
for ever and ever.
Let the heavens bless you
and all things you have made
for evermore.
It was you who created Adam,
you who created Eve his wife
to be his help and support;
and from these two the human race was born.
It was you who said,
'It is not good that the man should be alone;
let us make him a helpmate like himself.'
And so I do not take my sister
for any lustful motive;
I do in in singleness of heart.
Be kind enough to have pity on her and on me
and bring us to old age together."

6. *A reading from the Song of Solomon (2:8-10, 14, 16a;*
8:6-7a)

I hear my Beloved.
See how he comes
leaping on the mountains,
bounding over the hills.
My Beloved is like a gazelle,
like a young stag.
See where he stands
behind our wall.
He looks in at the window,
he peers through the lattice.
My Beloved lifts up his voice,
he says to me,

Note: This page is reproduced from the Couple's Book.

"Come then, my love,
my lovely one, come.
My dove, hiding in the clefts of the rock,
in the coverts of the cliff,
show me your face,
let me hear your voice;
for your voice is sweet
and your face is beautiful."
My Beloved is mine and I am his.
He said to me:
Set me like a seal on your heart,
like a seal on your arm.
For love is strong as Death,
jealousy relentless as Sheol.
The flash of it is a flash of fire,
a flame of Yahweh himself.
Love no flood can quench,
no torrents drown.

7. A reading from the book of Sirach (26:1-4, 16-21)

Happy the husband of a really good wife;
    the number of his days will be doubled.
A perfect wife is the joy of her husband,
    he will live out the years of his life in peace.
A good wife is the best of portions,
    reserved for those who fear the Lord;
rich or poor, they will be glad of heart,
    cheerful of face, whatever the season.

The grace of a wife will charm her husband,
    her accomplishments will make him the stronger.
A silent wife is a gift from the Lord,
    no price can be put on a well-trained character.
A modest wife is a boon twice over,
    a chaste character cannot be weighed on scales.
Like the sun rising over the mountains of the Lord
    is the beauty of a good wife in a well-kept house.

8. A reading from the book of the prophet Jeremiah (31:31-32a, 33-34a)

See, the days are coming—it is Yahweh who speaks—when I will make a new covenant with the House of Israel (and the House of Judah), but not a covenant like the one I made with their ancestors on the day I took them by the hand to bring them out of the land of Egypt.

No, this is the covenant I will make with the House of Israel when those days arrive—it is Yahweh who speaks. Deep within them I will plant my Law, writing it on their hearts. Then I will be their God and they shall be my people. There will be no further need for neighbor to try to teach neighbor, or brother to say to brother, "Learn to know Yahweh!" No, they will all know me, the least no less than the greatest—it is Yahweh who speaks.

Note: This page is reproduced from the Couple's Book.

Responsorial Psalm

In addition to the psalm (or part of psalm) you choose to include in your wedding liturgy, you also have to decide whether to have it read or sung. There are beautiful musical arrangements for some of these psalms and they can enrich your ceremony. Discuss this with your leader of song or parish music director and listen to some of the options. If you do choose to have it sung, remember to include the words in your liturgy booklet if you want the community to sing it. If you choose to have it read, think carefully about the reader. Psalms were written as poems or songs. Will your reader be able to read it that way? List your choice on your planning sheet along with the name of the reader or soloist.

---

1. *Ps. 33:12 and 18, 20-21, 22)*

R. **The earth is full of the goodness of the Lord.**
Happy the nation whose God is Yahweh,
the people he has chosen for his heritage,
But see how the eye of Yahweh is on those who fear him
on those who rely on his love.
R. **The earth....**

Our soul awaits Yahweh,
he is our help and shield;
our hearts rejoice in him,
we trust in his holy name.
R. **The earth....**

Yahweh, let your love rest on us
as our hope has rested in you.
R. **The earth....**

2. *Psalm 34:1-2, 3-4, 5-6, 7-8*

R. **I will bless the Lord at all times.**
Or: R. **Taste and see the goodness of the Lord.**
I will bless Yahweh at all times,
his praise shall be on my lips continually;
my soul glories in Yahweh,
let the humble hear and rejoice.
R. **I will bless the Lord at all times.**
　Or: R. **Taste and see the goodness of the Lord.**

Proclaim with me the greatness of Yahweh,
together let us extol his name.
I seek Yahweh, and he answers me
and frees me from all my fears.

R. **I will bless the Lord at all times.**
　Or: R. **Taste and see the goodness of the Lord.**
Every face turned to him grows brighter
and is never ashamed.
A cry goes up from the poor man, and Yahweh
hears, and helps him in all his troubles.
R. **I will bless the Lord at all times.**
　Or: R. **Taste and see the goodness of the Lord.**

The angel of Yahweh pitches camp
around those who fear him; and he keeps them safe.
How good Yahweh is—only taste and see!
Happy the man who takes shelter in him.
R. **I will bless the Lord at all times.**
　Or: R. **Taste and see the goodness of the Lord.**

3. *Psalm 103: 1-2, 8 and 13, 17-18a*

R. **The Lord is kind and merciful.**
　Or: R. **The Lord's kindness is everlasting to those who fear him.**
Bless Yahweh, my soul,
bless his holy name, all that is in me!
Bless Yahweh, my soul,
and remember all his kindnesses:
R. **The Lord....** Or: R. **The Lord's kindness....**

Yahweh is tender and compassionate,
slow to anger, most loving;
As tenderly as a father treats his children,
so Yahweh treats those who fear him.
R. **The Lord....** Or: R. **The Lord's kindness....**

Yet Yahweh's love for those who fear him

Note: This page is reproduced from the Couple's Book.

lasts from all eternity and for ever,
like his goodness to their children's children,
as long as they keep his covenant.
R. The Lord... Or: R. The Lord's kindness....

4. *Psalm 112:1-2, 3-4, 5-6, 7-8, 9*

R. Happy are those who do what the Lord commands.
    Or: R. Alleluia.
Happy the man who fears Yahweh
by joyfully keeping his commandments!
Children of such a man will be powers on earth,
descendants of the upright will always be blessed.
R. Happy are.... Or: R. Alleluia.

There will be riches and wealth for his family,
and his righteousness can never change.
For the upright he shines like a lamp in the dark,
he is merciful, tenderhearted, virtuous.
R. Happy are.... Or: R. Alleluia.

Interest is not charged by this good man,
he is honest in all his dealings.
Kept safe by virtue, he is ever steadfast,
and leaves an imperishable memory behind him;
R. Happy are.... Or: R. Alleluia.

with constant heart, and confidence in Yahweh,
he need never fear bad news.
Steadfast in heart he overcomes his fears:
in the end he will triumph over his enemies.
R. Happy are.... Or: R Alleluia.

Quick to be generous, he gives to the poor,
his righteousness can never change,
men such as this will always be honored.
R. Happy are.... Or: R Alleluia.

5. *Psalm 128:1-2,3,4-6*

R. Happy are those who fear the Lord.
    Or: R. See how the Lord blesses those who fear
    him.
Happy, all those who fear Yahweh
and follow in his paths.

You will eat what your hands have worked for,
happiness and prosperity will be yours.
R. Happy are.... Or: R. See how....

Your wife: a fruitful vine
on the inner walls of your house.
Your sons: round your table
like shoots round an olive tree.
R. Happy are.... Or: R. See how....

Such are the blessings that fall
on the man who fears Yahweh.
May Yahweh bless you from Zion
all the days of your life!
May you see Jerusalem prosperous
and live to see your children's children.
R. Happy are.... Or: R. See how....

6. *Psalm 145:8-9, 10 and 15, 17-18*

R. The Lord is compassionate to all his creatures.
He, Yahweh, is merciful, tenderhearted,
slow to anger, very loving,
and universally kind; Yahweh's tenderness
embraces all his creatures.
R. The Lord is compassionate to all his creatures.

Yahweh, all your creatures thank you,
and your faithful bless you.
Patiently all creatures look to you
to feed them throughout the year;
R. The Lord is compassionate to all his creatures.

Righteous in all that he does,
Yahweh acts only out of love,
standing close to all who invoke him,
close to all who invoke Yahweh faithfully.
R. The Lord is compassionate to all his creatures.

7. *Psalm 148:1-2, 3-4, 9-10, 11-12, 13*

R. Let all praise the name of the Lord.
    Or: Alleluia.
Let heaven praise Yahweh:
praise him, heavenly heights,
praise him, all his angels,

Note: This page is reproduced from the Couple's Book.

praise him, all his armies!
R Let all.... Or: R Alleluia.

Praise him, sun and moon,
praise him, shining stars,
praise him, highest heavens,
and waters above the heavens!
R. Let all.... Or: R. Alleluia.

Mountains and hills,
orchards and forests,
wild animals and farm animals,
snakes and birds.

R. Let all.... Or: R. Alleluia.

All kings on earth and nations,
princes, all rulers in the world,
young men and girls,
old people, and children too!
R. Let all.... Or: R. Alleluia.

Let them all praise the name of Yahweh,
for his name and no other is sublime,
transcending earth and heaven in majesty.
R. Let all.... Or: R. Alleluia.

Note: This page is reproduced from the Couple's Book.

Second Reading

The second Scripture reading is from the Christian Scriptures (New Testament). The following selections each have a specific theme. Select a reading that best fits what you want to say about your relationship with each other and with God, and again, be certain that it fits in with the theme of your liturgy. Record your selections and your reader(s) on your planning sheet.

---

1. A reading from the letter of Paul to the Romans (8:31b-35, 37-39)

With God on our side who can be against us? Since God did not spare his own Son, but gave him up to benefit us all, we may be certain, after such a gift, that he will not refuse anything he can give. Could anyone accuse those that God has chosen? When God acquits, could anyone condemn? Could Christ Jesus? No! He not only died for us—he rose from the dead, and there at God's right hand he stands and pleads for us.

Nothing therefore can come between us and the love of Christ, even if we are troubled or worried, or being persecuted, or lacking food or clothes, or being threatened or even attacked. These are the trials through which we triumph, by the power of him who loved us.

For I am certain of this: neither death nor life, no angel, no prince, nothing that exists, nothing still to come, not any power, or height or depth, nor any created thing, can ever come between us and the love of God made visible in Christ Jesus our Lord.

2. A reading from the letter from Paul to the Romans (12:1-2, 9-18 [longer])

Think of God's mercy, my brothers, and worship him, I beg you, in a way that is worthy of thinking beings, by offering your living bodies as a holy sacrifice, truly pleasing to God. Do not model yourselves on the behavior of the world around you, but let your behavior change, modeled by your new mind. This is the only way to discover the will of God and know what is good, what it is that God wants, what is the perfect thing to do.

Do not let your love be a pretense, but sincerely prefer good to evil. Love each other as much as brothers should, and have a profound respect for each other. Work for the Lord with untiring effort and with great earnestness of spirit. If you have hope, this will make you cheerful. Do not give up if trials come; and keep on praying. If any of the saints are in need you must share with them; and you should make hospitality your special care.

Bless those who persecute you: never curse them, bless them. Rejoice with those who rejoice and be sad with those in sorrow. Treat everyone with equal kindness; never be condescending but make real friends with the poor. Do not allow yourself to become self-satisfied. Never repay evil with evil but let everyone see that you are interested only in the highest ideals. Do all you can to live at peace with everyone.

2a. A reading from the letter of Paul to the Romans (12:1-2, 9-13 [shorter])

Think of God's mercy, my brothers, and worship him, I beg you, in a way that is worthy of thinking beings, by offering your living bodies as a holy sacrifice, truly pleasing to God. Do not model yourselves on the behavior of the world around you, but let your behavior change, modeled by your new mind. This is the only way to discover the will of God and know what is good, what it is that God wants, what is the perfect thing to do.

Do not let your love be a pretense, but sincerely prefer good to evil. Love each other as much as brothers should, and have a profound respect for each other. Work for the Lord with untiring effort and with great earnestness of spirit. If you have hope, this will make you cheerful. Do not give up if trials come; and keep on praying. If any of the saints are in need you must share with them; and you should make hospitality your special care.

100

Note: This page is reproduced from the Couple's Book.

3. A reading from the first letter of Paul to the Corinthians (6:13c-15a, 18-20)

The body—this is not meant for fornication; it is for the Lord, and the Lord for the body. God, who raised the Lord from the dead, will by his power raise us up too.

You know, surely, that your bodies are members making up the body of Christ?

But anyone who is joined to the Lord is one spirit with him.

Keep away from fornication. All the other sins are committed outside the body; but to fornicate is to sin against your own body. Your body, you know, is the temple of the Holy Spirit, who is in you since you received him from God. You are not your own property; you have been bought and paid for. That is why you should use your body for the glory of God.

4. A reading from the first letter of Paul to the Corinthians (12:31-13:1-8a)

Be ambitious for the higher gifts. And I am going to show you a way that is better than any of them.

If I have all the eloquence of men or angels, but speak without love, I am simply a gong booming or a cymbal clashing. If I have the gift of prophecy, understanding all the mysteries there are, and knowing everything, and if I have faith in all its fullness, to move mountains, but without love, then I am nothing at all. If I give away all that I possess, piece by piece, and if I even let them take away my body to burn it, but am without love, it will do me no good whatever.

Love is always patient and kind; it is never jealous; love is never boastful or conceited; it is never rude or selfish; it does not take offense, and is not resentful. Love takes no pleasure in other people's sins but delights in the truth; it is always ready to excuse, to trust, to hope, and to endure whatever comes. Love does not come to an end.

5. A reading from the letter of Paul to the Ephesians (5:2a, 21-33 [longer])

Follow Christ by loving as he loved you, giving himself up in our place.

Give way to one another in obedience to Christ. Wives should regard their husbands as they regard the Lord, since as Christ is head of the Church and saves the whole body, so is a husband the head of his wife; and as the Church submits to Christ, so should wives to their husbands, in everything. Husbands should love their wives just as Christ loved the Church and sacrificed himself for her to make her holy. He made her clean by washing her in water with a form of words, so that when he took her to himself she would be glorious, with no speck or wrinkle or anything like that, but holy and faultless. In the same way, husbands must love their wives as they love their own bodies; for a man to love his wife is for him to love himself. A man never hates his own body, but he feeds it and looks after it; and that is the way Christ treats the Church, because it is his body—and we are its living parts. *For this reason, a man must leave his father and mother and be joined to his wife, and the two will become one body.* This mystery has many implications; but I am saying it applies to Christ and the Church. To sum up; you too, each one of you, must love his wife as he loves himself; and let every wife respect her husband.

5a. A reading from the letter of Paul to the Ephesians (5:2a, 25-32 [shorter])

Follow Christ by loving as he loved you, giving himself up in our place.

Husbands should love their wives just as Christ loved the Church and sacrificed himself for her to make her holy. He made her clean by washing her in water with a form of words, so that when he took her to himself she would be glorious, with no speck or wrinkle or anything like that, but holy and faultless. In the same way, husbands must love their wives as they love their own bodies; for a man to love his wife is for him to love himself. A man never hates his own body, but he feeds it and looks after it; and that is the way Christ treats the Church,

---

101

Note: This page is reproduced from the Couple's Book.

because it is his body—and we are its living parts. *For this reason, a man must leave his father and mother and be joined to his wife, and the two will become one body.* This mystery has many implications; but I am saying it applies to Christ and the Church.

6. A reading from the letter of Paul to the Colossians (3:12-17)

You are God's chosen race, his saints; he loves you, and you should be clothed in sincere compassion, in kindness and humility, gentleness and patience. Bear with one another; forgive each other as soon as a quarrel begins. The Lord has forgiven you; now you must do the same. Over all these clothes, to keep them together and complete them, put on love. And may the peace of Christ reign in your hearts, because it is for this that you were called together as parts of one body. Always be thankful.

Let the message of Christ, in all its richness, find a home with you. Teach each other, and advise each other, in all wisdom. With gratitude in your hearts sing psalms and hymns and inspired songs to God; and never say or do anything except in the name of the Lord Jesus, giving thanks to God the Father through him.

7. A reading from the first letter of Peter (3:1-9)

Wives should be obedient to their husbands. Then, if there are some husbands who have not yet obeyed the word, they may find themselves won over, without a word spoken, by the way their wives behave, when they see how faithful and conscientious they are. Do not dress up for show: doing up your hair, wearing gold bracelets and fine clothes; all this should be inside, in a person's heart, imperishable: the ornament of a sweet and gentle disposition—this is what is precious in the sight of God. That was how the holy women of the past dressed themselves attractively—they hoped in God and were tender and obedient to their husbands; like Sarah, who was obedient to Abraham, and called him her *lord.* You are now her children, as long as you live good lives and do not give way to fear or worry.

In the same way, husbands must always treat their wives with consideration in their life together, respecting a woman as one who, though she may be the weaker partner, is equally an heir to the life of grace. This will stop anything from coming in the way of your prayers.

Finally: you should all agree among yourselves and be sympathetic; love the brothers, have compassion and be self-effacing. Never pay back one wrong with another, or an angry word with another one; instead, pay back with a blessing. That is what you are called to do, so that you inherit a blessing yourself.

8. A reading from the first letter of John (3:18-24)

My children, our love is not to be just words or
mere talk,
but something real and active;
only by this can we be certain
that we are children of the truth
and be able to quiet our conscience in his presence,
whatever accusations it may raise against us,
because God is greater than our conscience
and he knows everything.
My dear people,
if we cannot be condemned by our own conscience,
we need not be afraid in God's presence,
and whatever we ask him,
we shall receive,
because we keep his commandments
and live the kind of life that he wants.
His commandments are these:
that we believe in the name of his Son Jesus Christ
and that we love one another
as he told us to.
Whoever keeps his commandments
lives in God and God lives in him.
We know that he lives in us
by the Spirit that he has given us.

9. A reading from the first letter of John (4:7-12)

My dear people,
let us love one another
since love comes from God
and everyone who loves is begotten by God and
knows God.

Note: This page is reproduced from the Couple's Book.

Anyone who fails to love can never have known God,
because God is love.
God's love for us was revealed
when God sent into the world his only Son
so that we could have life through him;
this is the love I mean:
not our love for God,
but God's love for us when he sent his Son
to be the sacrifice that takes our sins away.
My dear people,
since God has loved so much,
we too should love one another.
No one has ever seen God;
but as long as we love one another
God will live in us
and his love will be complete in us.

10. A reading from the book of Revelation (19:1,5-9a)

I, John, seemed to hear the great sound of a huge crowd in heaven, singing, "Alleluia! Victory and glory and power to our God!" Then a voice came from the throne; it said, "Praise our God, you servants of his and all who, *great or small, revere him..*" And I seemed to hear the voices of a huge crowd, like the sound of the ocean or the great roar of thunder, answering, "Alleluia! The reign of the Lord our God Almighty has begun; let us be glad and joyful and give praise to God, because this is the time for the marriage of the Lamb. His bride is ready, and she has been able to dress herself in dazzling white linen, because her linen is made of the good deeds of the saints." The angel said, "Write this: Happy are those who are invited to the wedding feast of the Lamb."

103

Note: This page is reproduced from the Couple's Book.

Gospel Acclamation

With your readings selected, you now need to choose an introduction to the good news of Jesus. The Gospel acclamation announces that there is an important reading coming up. When reviewing the acclamations, therefore, select one that truly proclaims what is coming. Ask yourselves which of the following choices appropriately announces the Gospel and emphasizes what is important in our lives as a loving Christian couple?

The reader(s) of the second reading or the leader of song are usually the ones who read the acclamation. Remember to ask them to do this one too. Make sure the words are listed in your liturgy booklet. And list your choices on the planning sheet.

---

1. God is love;
   let us love one another as he has loved us.
   (1 John 4:8, 11)

2. If we love one another,
   God will live in us in perfect love. (1 John 4:12)

3. He who lives in love, lives in God,
   and God in him.
   (1 John 4:16)

4. Everyone who loves is born of God and knows him. (1 John 4:7b)

Note: This page is reproduced from the Couple's Book.

Gospel

In the Gospels, Matthew, Mark, Luke, and John wrote of the saving life and teachings of Jesus Christ. From the selections listed here, select the one that best expresses what you believe as a couple: about your relationship, your love, and the presence of God in your life together. List your selection on the planning sheet. Usually the priest presiding at your wedding reads the Gospel. However, if another priest is concelebrating, he may also be invited to read the Gospel. One further note: usually the person who reads the Gospel also gives a sermon, or homily. Discuss this with the priest as you plan. If a non-Catholic Christian minister is also taking part in the ceremony, he or she may, depending on the regulations of your diocese, proclaim the Gospel and/or deliver the homily. Confer with the priest about this.

---

1. A reading from the Holy Gospel according to Matthew (5:1-12a)

Seeing the crowds, Jesus went up the hill. There he sat down and was joined by his disciples. Then he began to speak. This is what he taught them:
"How happy are the poor in spirit;
theirs is the kingdom of heaven.
Happy the gentle:
they shall have the earth for their heritage.
Happy those who mourn:
they shall be comforted.
Happy those who hunger and thirst for what is right:
they shall be satisfied.
Happy the merciful:
they shall have mercy shown them.
Happy the pure in heart:
they shall see God.
Happy the peacemakers:
they shall be called sons of God.
Happy those who are persecuted in the cause of right:
theirs is the kingdom of heaven.
Happy are you when people abuse you and persecute you and speak all kinds of calumny against you on my account. Rejoice and be glad, for your reward will be great in heaven."

2. A reading from the Holy Gospel according to Matthew (5:13-16)

"You are the salt of the earth. But if salt becomes tasteless, what can make it salty again? It is good for nothing, and can only be thrown out to be trampled underfoot by men.
"You are the light of the world. A city built on a hilltop cannot be hidden. No one lights a lamp to put it under a tub; they put it on the lampstand where it shines for everyone in the house. In the same way your light must shine in the sight of men, so that, seeing your good works, they may give the praise to your Father in heaven."

3. A reading from the Holy Gospel according to Matthew (7:21, 24-29 [longer])

"It is not those who say to me, 'Lord, Lord,' who will enter the kingdom of heaven, but the person who does the will of my Father in heaven.
"Therefore, everyone who listens to these words of mine and acts on them will be like a sensible man who built his house on rock. Rain came down, floods rose, gales blew and hurled themselves against that house, and it did not fall: it was founded on rock. But everyone who listens to these words of mine and does not act on them will be like a stupid man who built his house on sand. Rain came down, floods rose, gales blew and struck that house, and it fell; and what a fall it had!"
Jesus had now finished what he wanted to say, and his teaching made a deep impression on the people because he taught them with authority, and not like their own scribes.

3a. A reading from the Holy Gospel according to Matthew (7:21, 24-25 [shorter])

Note: This page is reproduced from the Couple's Book.

"It is not those who say to me, 'Lord, Lord,' who will enter the kingdom of heaven, but the person who does the will of my Father in heaven.

"Therefore, everyone who listens to these words of mine and acts on them will be like a sensible man who built his house on rock. Rain came down, floods rose, gales blew and hurled themselves against that house, and it did not fall: it was founded on rock."

4. A reading from the Holy Gospel according to Matthew (19:3-6)

Some Pharisees approached Jesus, and to test him they said, "Is it against the Law for a man to divorce his wife on any pretext whatever?" He answered, "Have you not read that the creator from the beginning *made them male and female* and that he said: *This is why a man must leave father and mother, and cling to his wife, and the two become one body?* They are no longer two, therefore, but one body. So then, what God has united, man must not divide."

5. A reading from the Holy Gospel according to Matthew (22:35-40)

To disconcert Jesus, a lawyer put a question, "Master, which is the greatest commandment of the Law?" Jesus said, "*You must love the Lord your God with all your Heart, with all your soul, and with all your mind.* This is the greatest and the first commandment. The second resembles it: *You must love your neighbor as yourself.* On these two commandments hang the whole Law, and the Prophets also."

6. A reading from the Holy Gospel according to Mark (10:6-9)

From the beginning of creation God made them male and female. This is why a man must leave father and mother, and the two become one body. They are no longer two, therefore, but one body. So then, what God has united, man must not divide.

7. A reading from the Holy Gospel according to John (2:1-11)

There was a wedding at Cana in Galilee. The mother of Jesus was there, and Jesus and his disciples had also been invited. When they ran out of wine, since the wine provided for the wedding was all finished, the mother of Jesus said to him, "They have no wine." Jesus said, "Woman, why turn to me? My hour has not come yet." His mother said to the servants, "*Do whatever he tells you.*" There were six stone water jars standing there, meant for the ablutions that are customary among the Jews: each could hold twenty or thirty gallons. Jesus said to the servants, "Fill the jars with water," and they filled them to the brim. "Draw out some now," he told them, "and take it to the steward." They did this; the steward tasted the water, and it had turned into wine. Having no idea where it came from—only the servants who had drawn the water knew—the steward called the bridegroom and said, "People generally serve the best wine first, and keep the cheaper sort till the guests have had plenty to drink; but you have kept the best wine till now."

This was the first of the signs given by Jesus: it was given at Cana in Galilee. He let his glory be seen, and his disciples believed in him.

8. A reading from the Holy Gospel according to John (15:9-12)

"As the Father has loved me,
so I have loved you.
Remain in my love.
If you keep my commandments
you will remain in my love,
just as I have kept my Father's commandments
and remain in his love.
I have told you this
so that my own joy may be in you
and your joy be complete.
This is my commandment:
love one another,
as I have loved you."

106

Note: This page is reproduced from the Couple's Book.

9. A reading from the Holy Gospel according to John
(15:12-16)

"This is my commandment:
love one another,
as I have loved you.
A man can have no greater love
than to lay down his life for his friends.
You are my friends,
if you do what I command you.
I shall not call you servants anymore,
because a servant does not know
his master's business;
I call you friends,
because I have made known to you
everything I have learned from my Father.
You did not choose me,
no, I chose you;
and I commissioned you
to go out and to bear fruit,
fruit that will last;
and then the Father will give you
anything you ask him in my name."

10. A reading from the Holy Gospel according to John
(17:20-26 [longer])

I pray not only for these,
but for those also
who through their words will believe in me.
May they all be one.
Father, may they be one in us,
as you are in me and I am in you,
so that the world may believe it was you who sent
    me.
I have given them the glory you gave to me,
that they may be one as we are one.
With me in them and you in me,
may they be so completely one
that the world will realize that it was you who sent
    me

and that I have loved them as much as you loved
    me.
Father, I want those you have given me
to be with me where I am,
so that they may always see the glory
you have given me
because you loved me
before the foundation of the world.
Father, Righteous One,
the world has not known you,
but I have known you,
and these have known
that you have sent me.
I have made your name known to them
and will continue to make it known,
so that the love with which you loved me may be
    in them,
and so that I may be in them."

10a. A reading from the Holy Gospel according to John
(17:20-23 [shorter])

"I pray not only for these,
but for those also
who through their words will believe in me.
May they all be one.
Father, may they be one in us,
as you are in me and I am in you,
so that the world may believe it was you who sent
    me.
I have given them the glory you gave to me,
that they may be one as we are one.
With me in them and you in me,
may they be so completely one
that the world will realize that it was you who sent
    me
and that I have loved them as much as you loved
    me."

107

Note: This page is reproduced from the Couple's Book.

Rite of Marriage

Exchange of Wedding Vows

Introduction

Priest: My dear friends, you have come together in this church so that the Lord may seal and strengthen your love in the presence of the Church's minister and this community. Christ abundantly blesses this love. He has already consecrated you in baptism and now he enriches and strengthens you by a special sacrament so that you may assume the duties of marriage in mutual and lasting fidelity. And so, in the presence of the Church, I ask you to state your intentions.

Statement of Intentions

Priest: N. and N., have you come together freely and without reservation to give yourselves to each other in marriage?

Couple: We have.

Priest: Will you love and honor each other as man and wife for the rest of your lives?

Couple: We will.

Priest: Will you accept children lovingly from God and bring them up according to the law of Christ and his Church?

Couple: We will.

Consent

Priest: Since it is your intention to enter into marriage, join your right hands and declare your consent before God and his Church.

1. Groom: I, N. take you, N. to be my wife. I promise to be true to you in good times and in bad, in sickness and in health. I will love you and honor you all the days of my life.

Bride: I, N., take you, N. to be my husband. I promise to be true to you in good times and in bad, in sickness and in health. I will love you and honor you all the days of my life.

2. Priest: N., do you take N. to be your wife? Do you promise to be true to her in good times and in bad, in sickness and in health, to love her and honor her all the days of your life?

Groom: I do.

Priest: N., do you take N. to be your husband? Do you promise to be true to him in good times and in bad, in sickness and in health, to love him and honor him all the days of your life?

Bride: I do.

108

Note: This page is reproduced from the Couple's Book.

3. *Couple:* I, N., take you, N., for my lawful wife (husband), to have and to hold, from this day forward, for better, for worse, for richer, for poorer, in sickness and in health, until death do us part.

4. *Priest:* N., do you take N. for your lawful wife (husband), to have and to hold, from this day forward, for better, for worse, for richer, for poorer, in sickness and in health, until death do you part?

Bride/
Groom: I do.

Reception of Consent

Priest: You have declared your consent before the Church. May the Lord in his goodness strengthen your consent and fill you with his blessings. What God has joined, men must not divide.

All: Amen.

Note: This page is reproduced from the Couple's Book.

Blessing and Exchange of Rings

Most couples being married today have a two-ring blessing, each giving the other a ring to symbolize their marriage, love, and commitment. When selecting this blessing, read through them carefully, selecting the one that best expresses your love and your hopes. Add this decision to your planning sheet.

1. May the Lord bless these rings
   which you have given to each other
   as the sign of your love and fidelity.

2. Lord, bless and consecrate N. and N.
   in their love for each other.
   May these rings be a symbol
   of true faith in each other,
   and always remind them of their love.
   Through Christ our Lord.

3. Lord, bless these rings which we bless in your name.
   Grant that those who wear them
   may always have a deep faith in each other.
   May they do your will
   and always live together.
   (We ask this) through Christ our Lord.

Note: This page is reproduced from the Couple's Book.

Prayer of the Couple

Reciting this prayer as a couple is an option to consider. It usually would be said by the bride and groom after communion, during the time for meditation. While some couples may want to thank God in the presence of their family and friends, others prefer to do it privately. The choice is yours.

If you decide to have such a prayer, you can make it personal by writing it yourselves. It may be a prayer of thanksgiving for your love, for bringing you together, for your future, or for the loving support of your families and friends. You may seek guidance from God, and pray that God continue to bless each of you as wife and husband. There are countless ways to use this prayer, so be creative.

When you have written it, it would be advisable to have the priest or minister read through it so that they know what you intend to say. Remember to make note on your planning sheet that you are going to do the couple's prayer and attach a copy or two to it. When making arrangements at the rehearsal, make certain that you know where you intend to stand when you pray this prayer together and whether you will need a microphone. And practice it! Don't wait until the day of your wedding to do it for the first time.

Here are examples of a couple's prayer that you may use as a model. If you decide not to write your own, you may use these as they are.

---

1. *Couple:* Dear God, we give you thanks for creating each of us and for bringing us together in love. We ask you to bless us with health, happiness, and a long life together. We ask you to be with us during all the times of our marriage, both the good and the bad. Help us to always listen to each other, and treat each other with respect and tenderness. May we always know the joy and love that we feel today. Amen.

2. *Groom:* Lord, I thank you for (bride's name) who you have brought into my life. Help me to love her and be a good friend and husband to her. Help me to always be there for her, supporting her, listening to her, and sharing myself with her. And, if we are blessed by children, help me to be an example of love to them. Teach me how to be a father who loves and cares for his children, spends time with them, nurtures them, and teaches as well as learns from them.

   Bride: Lord, I thank you for (husband's name) whom you have brought into my life.

Help me to love him, support him, and care for him. Show me how to be his friend, his partner, his lover, and his wife. Help me to always listen to him and share myself with him. And if we are blessed by children, help me to be an example of love to them. Teach me to be a mother who cares for them, listens to them, plays with them, and nurtures them. Help us to share our love with them, and teach them to love themselves.

   Couple: We thank you, our loving God, for our families and friends. May we always feel their support in our lives and be their strength and encouragement. May you bless this wedding day as your Son blessed the wedding feast in Cana. Amen.

(Note: If your wedding is to take place within the Eucharistic liturgy, then continue with the next section. But if it is not, then turn to the planning section on the nuptial blessing.)

Note: This page is reproduced from the Couple's Book.

Prayer of the Faithful

When writing the petitions, take time to consider what you want to pray for. Most couples will include a prayer for their families, deceased loved ones, other married couples, the church community, world peace, or other particular concerns. Remember to ask the priest if he wants to write his own invitation to pray that begins the prayer, or whether he would like you to write it. Also select a response that you would like said after every petition and list it in your wedding booklet. You will also need to select someone to read these petitions. Make sure that they receive a copy of the petitions in advance to look over them. Here are some examples of petitions:

Priest: Creator God, giver of all life, You have brought us together today to celebrate the marriage of this couple. Hear now the concerns for which they pray...

1. Let us pray for peace in our world. May all people learn to respect each others differences, care for those in need, and live peacefully together. For this we pray...
Lord, hear our prayer.

2. Let us pray for the leaders of our world. May they make decisions based on love, working toward an end to injustice, poverty, and discrimination. For this we pray...
Lord, hear our prayer.

3. Let us pray for our families and friends. May they find love in their homes, fulfillment in their work, and contentment in their hearts. And may we be a source of strength to each other for years to come. For this we pray...
Lord, hear our prayer.

4. Let us pray for all married couples. May they always cherish their special love by respecting each other as individuals, trusting each other as friends, and honoring each other as partners. For this we pray...
Lord, hear our prayer.

5. Let us pray for (N.) and (N.). May their love deepen and grow as the years go by. May they find comfort in each others arms, support in each others eyes, and strength in the journey that they walk together. For this we pray...
Lord, hear our prayer.

6. Let us pray for our loved ones who have died. May their memories live on in our hearts. May we find comfort in sharing our stories of them with each other and find peace in knowing that they are in the company of God. For this we pray...
Lord, hear our prayer.

Priest: Let us pray. God of new life and love, hear the prayers of this couple. Be present to them in their life together as they learn to live in love. Touch their hearts, their minds, and their spirits. Bring healing to their injuries, strength to their weaknesses, and hopes to their dreams. We ask you this as a people who have followed our hearts and have found you. In Jesus' name we ask this. Amen.

Note: This page is reproduced from the Couple's Book.

Liturgy of the Eucharist

Prayer over the Gifts

While the priest prepares the bread and wine he offers a prayer over them. This is an appropriate time to offer your new marriage as a gift, asking God to watch over you and protect you. Record your choice on your planning sheet.

---

1. Lord, accept our offering
   for this newly married couple, N. and N.
   By your love and providence you have brought
   them together;
   now bless them all the days of their married life.
   (We ask this) through Christ our Lord.

2. Lord, accept the gifts we offer you
   on this happy day.
   In your fatherly love
   watch over and protect N. and N.,
   whom you have united in marriage.
   (We ask this) through Christ our Lord.

3. Lord, hear our prayers
   and accept the gifts we offer for N. and N.
   Today you have made them one in the sacrament of marriage.
   May the mystery of Christ's unselfish love,
   which we celebrate in this eucharist,
   increase the love for you and for each other.
   (We ask this) through Christ our Lord.

Note: This page is reproduced from the Couple's Book.

Preface

Each option for the preface expresses marriage in a different way. Select the one that fits your relationship and list it on your planning sheet. Make sure that your selection fits the theme you have chosen.

---

1. Father, all powerful and ever-living God,
   we do well always and everywhere to give you
      thanks.
   By this sacrament your grace unites man and
      woman
   in an unbreakable bond of love and peace.
   You have designed the chaste love of husband
      and wife
   for the increase both of the human family
   and of your own family born in baptism.

   You are the loving Father of the world of nature;
   you are the loving Father of the new creation of
      grace.
   In Christian marriage you bring together the
   two orders of creation:
   nature's gift of children enriches the world
   and your grace enriches also your Church.
   Through Christ the choirs of angels and all the
      saints
   praise and worship your glory.
   May our voices blend with theirs
   As we join in their unending hymn:

2. Father, all-powerful and ever-living God,
   we do well always and everywhere to give you
      thanks.

   You created man in love to share your divine
      life.
   We see his high destiny in the love of husband
      and wife,
   which bears the imprint of your own divine
      love.
   Love is man's origin,
   love is his constant calling,

love is his fulfillment in heaven.

The love of man and woman
is made holy in the sacrament of marriage,
and becomes the mirror of your everlasting love.

Through Christ the choirs of angels
and all the saints
praise and worship your glory.
May our voices blend with theirs
as we join in their unending hymn:

3. Father, all powerful and ever-loving God,
   we do well always and everywhere to give you
      thanks
   through Jesus Christ our Lord.
   Through him you entered into a new covenant
   with your people.
   You restored man to grace in the saving mystery
      of redemption.
   You gave him a share in the divine life
   through his union with Christ.
   You made him an heir of Christ's eternal glory.

   This outpouring of love in the new covenant of
      grace
   is symbolized in the marriage covenant
   that seals the love of husband and wife
   and reflects your divine plan of love.

   And so, with the angels and all the saints in
      heaven
   we proclaim your glory
   and join in their unending hymn of praise:

114

Note: This page is reproduced from the Couple's Book.

Nuptial Blessing

Throughout the liturgy there are two formal blessings of you as a newly married couple: the nuptial blessing and the final blessing. Select the nuptial blessing from the options here that best expresses your understanding of your marriage and your faith in God. List your choice on the planning sheet.

1. My dear friends, let us turn to the Lord and pray
that he will bless with his grace this woman (or N.)
now married in Christ to this man (or N.)
and that (through the sacrament of the body and
blood of Christ)
he will unite in love the couple he has joined
in this holy bond.

All pray silently for a short while. Then the priest extends his hands and continues:

Father, by your power you have made everything
out of nothing.
In the beginning you created the universe
and made mankind in your own likeness.
You gave man the constant help of woman
so that man and woman should no longer be two,
but one flesh,
and you teach us that what you have united
may never be divided.
Father, you have made the union of man and wife so
holy a mystery
that it symbolizes the marriage of Christ and his
Church.

Father, by your plan man and woman are united,
and married life has been established
as the one blessing that was not forfeited by original
sin
or washed away in the flood.
Look with love upon this woman, your daughter,
now joined to her husband in marriage.
She asks your blessing.
Give her the grace of love and peace.

May she always follow the example of the holy
women
whose praises are sung in the scriptures.
May her husband put his trust in her
and recognize that she is his equal

and the heir with him to the life of grace.
May he always honor her and love her
as Christ loves his bride, the Church.

Father, keep them always true to your commandments.
Keep them faithful in marriage
and let them be living examples of Christian life.

Give them the strength which comes from the gospel
so that they may be witnesses of Christ to others.
(Bless them with children
and help them to be good parents.
May they live to see their children's children.)
And, after a happy old age,
grant them fullness of life with the saints
in the kingdom of heaven.

(We ask this) through Christ our Lord.

2. Let us pray to the Lord for N. and N.
who come to God's altar at the beginning of their
married life
so that they may always be united in love for each
other
(as now they share in the body and blood of
Christ).

All pray silently for a short while. Then the priest extends his hands and continues:

Holy Father, you created mankind in your own image
and made man and woman to be joined as husband and wife
in union of body and heart
and so fulfill their mission in this world.
Father, to reveal the plan of your love,
you made the union of husband and wife

Note: This page is reproduced from the Couple's Book.

an image of the covenant between you and your people.

In the fulfillment of this sacrament,
the marriage of Christian man and woman
is a sign of the marriage between Christ and the Church.
Father, stretch out your hand, and bless N. and N.

Lord, grant that as they begin to live this sacrament
they may share with each other the gifts of your love
and become one in heart and mind
as witnesses to your presence in their marriage.
Help them to create a home together
(and give them children to be formed by the gospel
and to have a place in your family).

Give your blessings to N., your daughter,
so that she may be a good wife (and mother),
caring for the home, faithful in love for her husband,
generous and kind.
Give your blessings to N., your son,
so that he may be a faithful husband
(and a good father).

Father, grant that as they come together to your table on earth,
so they may one day have the joy of sharing your feast in heaven.
(We ask this) through Christ our Lord.

3. My dear friends, let us ask God
for his continued blessings upon this bridegroom

and his bride
(or N. and N.).

All pray silently for a short while. Then the priest extends his hands and continues:

Holy Father, creator of the universe,
maker of man and woman in your own likeness,
source of blessing for married life,
we humbly pray to you for this woman
who today is united with her husband in this sacrament of marriage.

May your fullest blessing come upon her and her husband
so that they may together rejoice in your gift of married love
(and enrich your Church with their children).

Lord, may they both praise you when they are happy
and turn to you in their sorrows.

May they be glad that you help them in their work
and know that you are with them in their need.
May they pray to you in the community of the Church,
and be your witnesses in the world.
May they reach old age in the company of their friends,
and come at last to the kingdom of heaven.

(We ask this) through Christ our Lord.

Note: This page is reproduced from the Couple's Book.

Prayer After Communion

Select one of these options and list it on your planning sheet.

1. Lord, in your love
   you have given us this eucharist
   to unite us with one another and with you.
   As you have made N. and N.
   one in this sacrament of marriage
   (and in the sharing of the one bread and the one
   cup),
   so now make them one in love for each other.
   (We ask this) through Christ our Lord.

2. Lord, we who have shared the food of your table
   pray for our friends N. and N.,
   whom you have joined together in marriage.

   Keep them close to you always.
   May their love for each other
   proclaim to all the world
   their faith in you.
   (We ask this) through Christ our Lord.

3. Almighty God,
   may the sacrifice we have offered
   and the eucharist we have shared
   strengthen the love of N. and N.,
   and give us all your fatherly aid.
   (We ask this) through Christ our Lord.

Note: This page is reproduced from the Couple's Book.

Final Blessing

In this, the second formal blessing of you as a newly married couple, the priest offers a prayer for you as your wedding liturgy comes to an end and you are about to embark on your life together as husband and wife. Select the one you want and list it on your planning sheet.

---

1. God the eternal Father keep you in love with each other,
so that the peace of Christ may stay with you
and be always in your home.

R. Amen.

May (your children bless you,)
your friends console you
and all men live in peace with you.

R. Amen.

May you always bear witness to the love of God in this world
so that the afflicted and the needy
will find in you generous friends,
and welcome you into the joys of heaven.

R. Amen.

And may almighty God bless you all,
the Father, and the Son, and the Holy Spirit.

R. Amen.

2. May God, the almighty Father,
give you his joy
and bless you (in your children).

R. Amen.

May the only Son of God have mercy on you
and help you in good times and in bad.

R. Amen.
May the Holy Spirit of God
always fill your hearts with his love.

R. Amen.

3. May the Lord Jesus, who was a guest at the wedding in Cana, bless you and your families and friends.

R. Amen.

May Jesus, who loved his Church to the end,
always fill your hearts with his love.

R. Amen.

May he grant that, as you believe in his resurrection,
so you may wait for him in joy and hope.

R. Amen.

And may almighty God bless you all,
the Father, and the Son, and the Holy Spirit.

R. Amen.

4. May almighty God, with his words of blessing,
unite your hearts in the never-ending bond of pure love.

R. Amen.

May your children bring you happiness, and may your generous
love for them be returned to you, many times over.

R. Amen.

May the peace of Christ live always in your hearts and in your home.
May you have true friends to stand by you, both in joy and in sorrow.
May you be ready and willing to help and com-

Note: This page is reproduced from the Couple's Book.

fort all who come to you in need.
And may the blessings promised to the compassionate be yours in abundance.

May you find happiness and satisfaction in your work.
May daily problems never cause you undue anxiety, nor the
desire for earthly possessions dominate your lives.
But may your hearts' first desire be always the good things waiting
for you in the life of heaven.

R. Amen.

May the Lord bless you with many happy years together,
so that you may enjoy the rewards of a good life.
And after you have served him loyally in his kingdom on earth,
may he welcome you to his eternal kingdom in heaven.

R. Amen.

119

Note: This page is reproduced from the Couple's Book.

Resources

This resource appendix contains an assortment of resources, some of which are hotline numbers for immediate help, and others are for information or referrals. The best way to obtain assistance for yourself or for a loved one is to look for services in your immediate area. Look in your local telephone book or call the Catholic social agency/services number for information. If they are unable to help you, the following list may assist you in reaching help.

One final note, there is nothing here about marriage or family therapy or counseling. We recommend that you seek this locally if you and your partner are experiencing trouble in your relationship. Remember, it's better to seek help early in the problem, rather than wait until it's too late.

Al-Anon Family Group Headquarters
800-356-9996

Alcoholics Anonymous
No national phone number. Check local area.

Center for Disease Control
National AIDS Hotline 800-342-AIDS

Child Help Hotline
800-422-4453

Children of Alcoholics Foundation, Inc.
212-754-0656
Cocaine 1-800-262-2463

Diocesan Development Program for Natural Family Planning
3211 4th St., N.E.
Washington, D.C. 20017-1194
202-541-3240

Gamblers Anonymous
No national phone number. Check local area.

Narcotics Anonymous
No national phone number. Check local area.

National Association of Children of Alcoholics
Suite B
31582 Coast Highway
South Laguna, CA 92677
714-499-3889

National Clearing House for Alcohol and Drug Information
1-800-729-6686

National Coalition Against Sexual Assault
202-483-7165

National Domestic Violence Hotline
800-333-7233

National Institute on Drug Abuse:
Drug Information and Treatment Referral Program
800-662-HELP

120

Note: This page is reproduced from the Couple's Book.

Overeaters Anonymous
No national phone number. Check local area.

Parents Anonymous
22330 Hawthorne
Torrance, CA 90505
800-421-0353

Resolve (infertility support)
617-623-0744

Sex Addicts Anonymous
P.O. Box 3038
Minneapolis, MN 55403
612-339-0217

Sexaholics Anonymous
P.O. Box 300
Simi Valley, CA 93062
818-704-9854

Sex and Love Addicts Anonymous
P.O. Box 1964
Boston, MA 02105
617-625-7961

Sexually Transmitted Disease (STD) Hotline
800-227-8922

The Stepfamily Association of America
215 Centennial Mall South #212
Lincoln, NE 68508
402-477-7837

121

Note: This page is reproduced from the Couple's Book.

Of Related Interest...

Making Your Marriage Work
Growing in Love After Falling in Love
Christopher C. Reilly

This book is filled with practical, insightful ideas to stimulate a constructive and inspiring marriage.
ISBN: 0-89622-387-6, 180 pp, $7.95

Ecumenical Marriage & Remarriage
Gifts and Challenges to the Churches
Michael Lawler

The author challenges churches to recognize the gift of grace inherent in couples involved in both ecumenical marriages and in remarriages.
ISBN: 0-89622-441-4, 112 pp, $8.95

Secular Marriage, Christian Sacrament
Michael Lawler

This book analyzes the tradition of Christian marriage and seeks to uncover the essence of a Christian marriage.
ISBN: 0-89622-273-x, 192 pp, $8.95

What Women Don't Understand About Men*
*and vice versa
John Carmody

Here is an honest, open discussion between a man and a woman that explores the different approaches the sexes take to certain life situations.
ISBN: 0-89622-500-3, 112 pp, $7.95

We Celebrate Our Marriage
John and Laurie van Bemmel

Stories of married life in this booklet help spouses share their love and devotion.
ISBN: 0-89622-304-3, 32 pp, $1.95

Available at religious bookstores or from

TWENTY-THIRD PUBLICATIONS
P.O. Box 180
Mystic, CT 06355
1-800-321-0411